The Suicide Funeral
(or Memorial Service)

The Suicide Funeral (or Memorial Service)

Honoring Their Memory, Comforting Their Survivors

EDITED BY

MELINDA MOORE
RABBI DANIEL A. ROBERTS

Foreword by
Robert F. Morneau

RESOURCE *Publications* · Eugene, Oregon

THE SUICIDE FUNERAL (OR MEMORIAL SERVICE)
Honoring Their Memory, Comforting Their Survivors

Resource Publications
An Imprint of Wipf and Stock Publishers
199 W. 8th Ave., Suite 3
Eugene, OR 97401

www.wipfandstock.com

PAPERBACK ISBN: 978-1-4982-8958-0
HARDCOVER ISBN: 978-1-4982-8960-3
EBOOK ISBN: 978-1-4982-8959-7

Manufactured in the U.S.A.   MAY 9, 2017

Biblical translations follow the New American Bible unless otherwise noted.

Cultivating Connection, Compassion, and Confidence in Goodness: While Healing After Suicide by Bhikshuni Thubten Chodron used with permission.

Healing After Suicide by Bhikshuni Thubten Chodron used with permission.

The Selected Poetry of Jessica Powers,
Published by ICS Publications, Washington, D.C.
All copyrights, Carmelite Monastery, Pewaukee, WI. Used with permission

To clergy and religious leaders of all faiths
who honor with dignity and respect
those who have died by their own hand
and who lovingly minister to those touched by this loss.

Contents

CONTENTS

Poems

KRISTEN SPEXARTH

What Does it Mean

What is it about the phrase
'committed suicide'?
Why not say, 'she committed love' or
'he committed laughter'?
Words uttered from mouths removed
having never tasted it
wreck a curious kind of havoc
in the heart of many a survivor.
And the breach that causes such offense
along with the need to stigmatize
is it not more insult to our vanity
more reminder of our frailty
than offense to humanity?
To die of affliction
like any ailing body
tattered, torn, on the brink
beyond finding any link
so wracked with pain
no option remains but we

in horror that life could so test
and terrified of who might be next
shrink away, heaping judgments
on all who've left
crossing a border, taboo.
And I ask you
when does one 'commit' the act?
How do we read the walking dead
turning away from the fullness of longing
that signifies a life?
And how to read the random stuffing
heady diversions
walls we build around our hearts,
these various numbings we engage
hoping to soften the edge of pain
part of the human condition.

The Garden

A big stack of dishes takes time to do
so I take the time to do it
and building a garden or raising a child
is a labor of love that never ends
so I give ample room in my life
to the living heart of me.
The familiar we accommodate
as we go about planning our lives
but how many are prepared
to make room for a grief
like the untimely loss of a love?
And how long does it take
and what space do we make
after sharing a lifetime to leave it?

Every part of your day affected
from the way you wake to going to bed
when you love someone they are part of you
your every movement linked so deep you don't think it.
It just is, like they are, and surely will always be.
But people go
in untimely and tragic ways
leaving us to grieve
a loss so large most cannot conceive it.
And yet, there it is
and here we are
gathering days in bunches like bouquets
as we sit in stunned silence
numb to ourselves and to each other
numb to the dishes and the garden
unable to move and barely to breathe
this grieving is work like digging ditches
and it takes all my strength just to sit.
I don't understand this, I'm still new
but it's pretty clear that one year or two
will not get me through.
And I have a feeling that this loss is living
like a garden that needs my attention
and the space I must make to live with death
will require a daily commitment.
Don't fear you may remind me causing more pain
there is no moment I forget.
In fact, the opposite is true.
If you can join me in my garden, grieving,
together we may find a healing.

Bibliography

Spexarth, Kristen. *Passing Reflections, Volume III: Surviving Suicide Loss Through Mindfulness*. San Francisco: Big Think Media, 2016.

Contributors

Fr. William J. Bausch is a retired priest in the Diocese of Trenton, N.J. He is the author of over twenty books on parish life, spirituality, homiletics, and storytelling. He is also a popular worship leader and seminar presenter.

Kate Braestrup is an accidental chaplain. Her husband, Drew, a Maine state trooper, died in a car accident when he was considering a second career as an ordained minister. After her shock subsided, Braestrup decided to follow in his footsteps and became a chaplain for the Maine Warden Service. She is also the author of several books.

Venerable Thubten Chodron was ordained as a Buddhist nun in 1977 by Kyabje Ling Rinpoche in Dharamsala, India, and in 1986, she received *bhikshuni* (full) ordination in Taiwan. She studied and practiced Buddhism of the Tibetan tradition for many years in India and Nepal under the guidance of His Holiness the Dalai Lama, Tsenzhap Serkong Rinpoche, Zopa Rinpoche and other Tibetan masters. Seeing the importance and necessity of a monastery for Westerners training in the Tibetan Buddhist tradition, she founded Sravasti Abbey, a Buddhist monastic community in Washington, and is currently the abbess there.

Father John Colbert was awarded his PhD from the University of Fribourg in Switzerland, completing his dissertation on the theology of virtue in the thought of Thomas Aquinas. He joined the Pontifical Faculty of the Immaculate Conception in the Fall of 1998.

Rev. Karen Covey-Moore has been an ordained United Methodist minister since 1985. She has served churches throughout the Peninsula-Delaware Conference of The United Methodist Church as a pastor, two years as the pediatric chaplain of the Medical Center of Delaware, and three years as a bereavement counselor for Delaware Hospice. She is the co-founder of Healing Hearts Ministries: Ministry to Survivors of Suicide.

Sister Ann Davies is a Roman Catholic nun living in England who conducts civil funerals. She is the author of two books, *Shades of Suicide* and *Meditations for the Bereaved*.

Dr. Kenneth J. Doka is a Professor of Gerontology at the Graduate School of The College of New Rochelle and Senior Consultant to the Hospice Foundation of America. A prolific author, Dr. Doka was elected President of the Association for Death Education and Counseling in 1993. In 1995, he was elected to the Board of Directors of the International Work Group on Dying, Death, and Bereavement and served as chair from 1997–1999. Doka has keynoted conferences throughout North America as well as Europe, Asia, Australia, and New Zealand. He participates in the annual Hospice Foundation of America Teleconference and has appeared on CNN and *Nightline*. Dr. Doka is an ordained Lutheran minister.

Daymond Duck was born in 1939 at Trimble, Tennessee. At the age of forty, he entered the United Methodist Pastors ministry. He is a bivocational pastor, a prophecy conference speaker, a member of the Pre-Trib Study Group in Washington, D.C., and he preaches revivals. He is also the best-selling author of a shelf full of books.

Rev. Ron Edmondson is the senior pastor of Immanuel Baptist Church, Lexington, Kentucky.

Rabbi Ted Falcon was ordained in 1968 at the Hebrew Union College—Jewish Institute of Religion in Cincinnati, Ohio. He served in Los Angeles as a congregational and then a campus rabbi. In 1975, he earned a doctorate in Professional Psychology, with research focused on the nature of meditative and mystical states of consciousness. Since then, his work has bridged the psychological and the spiritual, encouraging deeper integration for greater freedom of personal action and understanding.

Dr. Earl A. Grollman a pioneer in the field of crisis intervention, was rabbi of the Beth El Temple Center in Belmont, Massachusetts for thirty-six years, and is a past president of Massachusetts Board of Rabbis. He is a certified Death Educator and Counselor and was a founder of the Good Grief Program that provides crisis intervention to schools and community groups to help children and adolescents when a friend, teacher, or parent is terminally ill or dies.

Rabbi Chaya Gusfield, ordained in the Jewish Renewal Movement in 2006, completed her Spiritual Direction training in 2001, and is a Board Certified Chaplain with the Association of Professional Chaplains. She has a long association serving many Bay Area synagogues including her home community Kehilla Community Synagogue and Beth Chaim Congregation. Rabbi Gusfield currently serves as a Palliative Care and Acute Care Chaplain for Kaiser Oakland/Richmond and recently served as the Jewish Chaplain for Alta Bates Summit Medical Center.

Rabbi Lori Klein is the Director of the Spiritual Care Service at Stanford Health Care. She served as the Cancer Care Chaplain there for more than seven years. She is also a spiritual leader in Santa Cruz, California. She received ordination through the ALEPH Rabbinical Program in 2006.

Rabbi Adam J. Raskin has been the spiritual leader of Congregation Har Shalom in Potomac, Maryland since 2011. Originally from Cleveland, Ohio, he was ordained at the Jewish Theological Seminary in New York and Jerusalem.

Father Ron Rolheiser MA, MRSc., PhD/STD, entered the priesthood in 1972. In 1998, Fr. Ron was elected Regional Councilor for Canada, serving on the General Administration of the Missionary Oblates of Mary Immaculate in Rome for six years. In 2005, Fr. Ron became the President of the Oblate School of Theology in San Antonio Texas, a position he maintains to this day.

Rev. Charles T. Rubey has been an archdiocesan priest for forty-eight years and has worked for Catholic Charities for forty-two years. He is the founder and director of the LOSS (Loving Outreach to Survivors of Suicide) program, which offers hope and healing to those who mourn a loss from suicide. Fr. Rubey has worked for thirty-five years with individuals who are grieving as a result from suicide.

Dr. Holly Toensing is assistant professor in the department of theology at Xavier University in Cincinnati. A New Testament scholar, she is also program chair for the Society of Biblical Literature's LGBTQ Hermeneutics Consultation.

Pastor Don Mackenzie, PhD, living in Minneapolis, is devoting himself to interfaith work after retiring as Minister and Head of Staff at Seattle's University Congregational United Church of Christ. Previously, he served congregations in Hanover, New Hampshire, and Princeton, New Jersey. Ordained in 1970, he is a graduate of Macalester College, Princeton Theological Seminary, and New York University.

Bishop Robert Morneau is a retired American prelate of the Roman Catholic Church who served as an auxiliary bishop of the Diocese of Green Bay. Father Morneau became an Auxiliary Bishop on February 22, 1979. He was one of the first American priests to be named a bishop by Pope John Paul II. Through the years, he has served the Diocese as a member of the College of Consultors and the Diocesan Finance Council; as the Vicar for Priests and the Vicar General; and as pastor of Resurrection Parish in Allouez. He studied at St. Norbert College and Sacred Heart Seminary before earning his bachelor's and master's degrees from Catholic University of America in Washington, D.C. A poet and author, he has written a number of books, including A New Heart: Eleven Qualities of Holiness, Notes of Thanksgiving: Notes to My Spiritual Teachers, and The Color of Gratitude: And Other Spiritual Surprises.

Diann L. Neu is cofounder and co-director of WATER, the Women's Alliance for Theology, Ethics and Ritual, 8121 Georgia Avenue, Suite 310, Silver Spring, MD, dneu@hers.com.

Jamal Rahman is a popular speaker on Islam, Sufi spirituality, and interfaith relations. He is the author of numerous books, including The Eye-Opening, Hope-Filled Friendship of a Pastor, a Rabbi, and an Imam. Jamal's passion lies in interfaith community building. He remains rooted in his Islamic tradition and cultivates "spaciousness" by being open to the beauty and wisdom of other faiths. By authentically and appreciatively understanding other paths, Jamal feels that he becomes a better Muslim. This spaciousness is not about conversion but about completion.

Harold Ivan Smith is a bereavement specialist on the teaching faculties of Saint Luke's Hospital, Kansas City, Missouri. He earned his doctorate from Asbury Theological Seminary. Smith has written 12 books on bereavement, including *Grief Keeping: Learning How Long Grief Lasts* and *Borrowed Narratives: Using Historical and Biographical Narratives with the Bereaving.* He frequently presents at conferences for bereavement, hospice, and funeral service. He is a Fellow in Thanatology recognized by the Association for Death Education and Counseling.

Terry L. Smith, EdD, LCSW is Chair of the Department of Behavioral Sciences and Social Work Program Director at Harding University, Searcy, Arkansas. Dr. Smith is a member of ADEC and American Academy of Bereavement.

Rev. Dennis Spence is the pastor of First United Methodist Church in Monticello, Arkansas.

Rev. Paul Tunkle embarked on his own spiritual journey in adulthood, which ultimately led him to a career in the Episcopal ministry. He has worked as a rector in churches in New Jersey, Louisiana, Maryland, and Maine. The single most defining experience of his life was the tragic death by suicide of his daughter, Lea, in 1997. In his crisis of faith, Tunkle came to a new understanding of the Scriptures, which ultimately strengthened his belief. He has used his experience to help others in emotional and spiritual crisis.

Anne Cronin Tyson is a Roman Catholic Spiritual Director who has been involved in suicide prevention efforts at the local, regional, state, national, and international levels. She is the cofounder with *Rev. Karen Covey-Moore* of Healing Hearts Ministries, a retreat ministry to those bereaved by suicide and also workshops for clergy and clinicians working with survivors. She is bereaved by her son, niece, and uncle's deaths by suicide.

Bishop William Young is the senior pastor of The Healing Center Full Gospel Baptist Church in Memphis, Tennessee.

Foreword

MOST REVEREND ROBERT F. MORNEAU
Auxiliary Bishop of Green Bay

The phone rang at 3:25 AM on April 26, 1990. No one wants a call in the middle of the night. As I picked up the receiver, my thoughts turned to my brother, who was dying from a brain tumor. The doctors gave him nine months to live, and he was now in the seventh month. I was sure that the sad news of his death was being delivered.

Wrong! The call came from my brother-in-law, whose daughter, my niece, had taken an overdose. The doctors were unable to save her. They desperately tried to pump her stomach, but the pills had done their mortal damage. She was but seventeen years of age and now, through suicide, had left her family in the darkness of grief and with that unanswerable question, *why?*

As I sank into a chair, I recalled a reflection of Albert Schweitzer, the medical doctor who served the poor in Africa for over fifty years. His observation, *there may have been smiles across a streetcar aisle that stayed the purpose of a suicide.* A small act of kindness to an absolute stranger has the potential to affirm existence and prevent a self-destructive act. Surely, my niece was smiled at, loved, and cared for. Why did this active concern not stay her suicide? What prevented her from embracing the golden fact that she was loved?

We are all pilgrims, indeed, struggling pilgrims on this perilous journey called life. We do not know the load that people carry, be it an abused childhood, guilt arising out of sin, a psychological temperament wrestling with chaotic, uncontrollable moods, an unrequited love. We are all in the same canoe, the same human condition in that everyone, without exception, experiences emotional distress of varying degrees, intellectual limitations that often blind us to the truth, and, yes, religious and philosophical aridity that questions the existence of God and the meaning of life.

Our participation in the solidarity of humankind should be a source of compassion. All of us have our dark days. Some of us have to deal with black holes, those horrendous abysses that speak of nothingness. If we have any sensitivity at all regarding our common human condition, it will eradicate judgmentalism and condemnation from our souls—*there but for the grace of God.*As a single human family, we are challenged to rejoice with those who rejoice and to weep with those who experienced loss and sorrow.

Over thirty years ago, I wrote an article entitled "The Healing Power of Poetry." I argued that poetry connects us with others, provides perspective and images to govern our days, refreshes and often refines the soul. Nelson Mandela, during his twenty-seven-year imprisonment in South Africa, found great strength and healing in memorizing William Ernest Henley's poem "Invictus." Poetry gave him the strength to endure years of deprivation and cruelty. That poem gave Mandela a vision and an ideal that made him *unconquerable.*

But is poetry healing for everyone? A former teacher of mine read my article on poetry and healing and simply responded, *if poetry is so healing, why then do so many poets—Sylvia Plath, Anne Sexton, John Berryman— take their own life?* I was unable to answer the question, but deep down, I still feel that poetry, music, and art have a way of sustaining human life and enriching it. Yes, it may well have the power to prevent suicide.

Several years ago, I read the memoirs of Kay Redfield Jamison, an American clinical psychologist and an expert on the topic of manic-depression. *An Unquiet Mind* (1995) traces her own bipolar disorder, and in that work, Jamison stresses the importance of strong relationships, hard work, and proper medication. Four years later, she wrote *Night Falls Fast: Understanding Suicide* (1999), a major study on the causes and motivations of suicide. Jamison herself had attempted suicide. Her writings have a deep realism because of her personal struggles with depression/despair. Anyone wanting a deeper understanding of self-destructive behavior would benefit greatly by reading Jamison's works.

Another individual, Walker Percy, a southern Catholic novelist and essayist, had to struggle with the issue of suicide. Both his grandfather and his father took their own lives, and, possibly, his mother's fatal car accident also was a suicide. The way that Percy dealt with those tragedies was to write about them in his novels, offering an interpretation and concluding that suicide was a *waste*. Whatever the reason, suicide availed nothing and did no good to anyone. Percy realized that the history of manic-depression was in his bloodstream, and he had to wrestle with the questions of life's meaning throughout his life. He was able, through discipline and grace, to conquer the demons of self-destruction.

Suicide is not a new phenomenon. The question of meaning and meaninglessness is not simply a contemporary concern. Every age and every culture has to contend with the big questions of identity, destiny, and ethics: Who are we? Where are we going? How do we get there? When answers are not available, illness quickly follows. Carl J. Jung knew this: "Meaninglessness inhibits fullness of life and is therefore equivalent to illness."[1] In writing *Hamlet*, Shakespeare knew this with his famous, *to be or not to be, that is the question*. But this is to suggest that people who are dealing with the question of living or dying are philosophical in nature, and so it might be. But there is another possibility, the loss of perspective.

What can too easily happen in our lives is that we *absolutize* a particular action or relationship. We make the part the whole and become unable to see the larger picture. This can throw a person into that dark hole where there appears to be no light at the end of the tunnel. The part becomes the whole, and there is nothing else.

This *absolutizing* was captured well in a poem by Jessica Powers:[2]

The Tear in the Shade

> I tore the new pale window shade with slightly
> more than a half-inch tear.
> I knew the Lady would be shocked to see
> what I had done with such finality.
> I went outside to lose my worry there.

---

1. Jung, *Memories, Dreams, Reflections*, 340

2. From The *Selected Poetry of Jessica Powers* published by ICS Publication, Washington, D.C., All copyrights, Carmelite Monastery, Pewaukee, WI. Used with permission. 1989.

Later when I came back into the room
it seemed that nothing but the tear was there.
There had been furniture, a rug, and pictures,
and on the table flowers in purple bloom.
It was amazing how they dwindled, dwindled,
and how the tear grew till it filled the room.[3]

Much help is needed in dealing with the issue of suicide at the pastoral level. The trauma that suicide survivors go through is incredibly painful. In this volume, *The Suicide Funeral*, counselors and pastors and scholars share their experience and perspective on this most difficult topic. Obviously, there are no *answers*, but there are frameworks for talking about and talking through the mystery of self-destruction. In her 1969 book *On Death and Dying*, Dr. Elisabeth Kubler-Ross rendered a great service in delineating the grief. This current volume attempts to delineate aspects of loss in the case of suicide and how we might respond to the needs of survivors. This work is ecumenical in nature, drawing from different religious and psychological traditions. In many cases, the authors have had personal experience of family members or close friends who have taken their lives. Thus, the essays are not abstract reflections but flow out of personal suffering and grief.

The highest form of knowledge is to know that we are surrounded by mystery, another insight from Dr. Albert Schweitzer. There are few mysteries greater than that of death, especially death that is the result of suicide. Thus, the warning of St. Bernard of Clairvaux deserves our attention, *be cautious in stepping into mysteries*. Well, the authors of this volume have taken the risk and stepped into the mystery of death. We should be grateful to them for this courage; we should be grateful to them for the wisdom that they share.

Bibliography

Powers, Jessica. *The Selected Poetry of Jessica Powers*. Washington, D.C.: ICS Publications, 1989.

---

3. Powers, *Selected Poems*, 118

Preface

In Tribute to Reverend James T. Clemons, PhD

Melinda Moore, PhD

This book would never have happened if it were not for the vision and tenacity of Rev. Jim Clemons. When you say the name "Jim Clemons," you rarely get a neutral response. Usually, it is a reverential nod of the head and an *oh, yes, I met him once*. Or, if someone knew Jim really well, it is a chuckle and a funny story about how he got you to do something you didn't want to do. Jim was persuasive and compelling and knew how to command a crowd as deftly as he knew how to maneuver working through an individual's resistance to helping him fight his next big cause or work on his next big project. Jim was a consummate Southern gentleman. He hailed from Arkansas and started his early career at Hendricks College, which he mentioned frequently with great affection. He became an ordained Methodist minister and a Civil Rights advocate. His intellectual rigor led him to Duke University, where he earned his PhD in Biblical Studies. He was a scholar, spending his summers in Greece and elsewhere conducting serious research. Jim taught many clergy—from many different faiths—at Wesley Theological Seminary in Washington, DC for decades. He touched the minds of thousands of clergy and seminarians. That is dwarfed by the lives he touched in his work in suicide prevention. Somewhere along the way, Jim discovered the enormous dearth of resources for those who were suffering, either from a suicide attempt or from having lost a loved one to suicide. Among the other books that he has written, he wrote the seminal, *What the Bible Says About Suicide,* the only text that addressed what the bible did and did not say on the topic. This was joined by *Sermons on Suicide* and *Children of Jonah.* In his retirement, Jim founded the Organization for Attempters and Survivors of Suicide in Interfaith Services (OASSIS) in 1997 and was president of the organization until 2006.

It was 2005 when Jim and Jerry Reed, Executive Director of the Suicide Prevention Action Network (SPAN–USA), conceptualized the first ever Suicide Attempt Conference in Memphis, Tennessee to be sponsored by OASSIS and SPAN USA. Charlie Curie, the Director of the federal Substance Abuse and Mental Health Services Administration (SAMHSA), had recently elevated suicide prevention to one of SAMHSA's top priorities and graciously agreed to underwrite the costs of the conference. This was an unheard of undertaking, but Jim knew the right people to lean on and get it done. I worked for Jerry Reed as a special projects manager and was tasked to help with the conference. That began a relationship of Jim having inspired ideas and convincing me to join his mission. Jim became my friend, my mentor, my occasional guest over lunch or dinner, and house guest. Jim's aesthetic was elevated. He loved fine dining and inspired people. He loved nature and all animals. He loved listening to opera during meals and especially loved the broadcast of the Metropolitan Opera on Saturdays. No one spoke more lovingly of his family—his wife, Barbara, and children, Tom and Margaret—than Jim. I will cherish those memories and also hold onto the inspiration of his ideas. His missions were prescient undertakings, and, in the midst of my work at SPAN and then my doctoral studies at Catholic University of America, I agreed to help him write and edit a book dedicated to creating template homilies and sermons to assist clergy in conducting the most unthinkable of services, *The Suicide Funeral.* Jim conceptualized and co-wrote the first draft of Chapter One, as well as other parts of the book. He recruited clergy to write the perspectives and service material. He had many ambitious ideas for this book. When Jim died unexpectedly in a train accident on January 14, 2011, the devastation of his death and the overwhelming nature of such a project forced me to shelve this book project. Several years later, feeling the hand of Jim urging me to press on, I became acquainted with Rabbi Daniel Roberts, who is an esteemed faith leader, Thanatologist, author, and suicide bereaved by his father's death. I knew I found the collaborator who I would complete this task with and would bring this effort home. I can see Jim smiling down now and in his gentle, southern lilt saying, "Well, friend, I'm so glad we met."

Our Mission

To our knowledge, nothing with *The Suicide Funeral (or Memorial Service): Honoring Their Memory, Comforting Their Survivors'* scope and depth has ever been published. This is an aid to anyone who will be called upon to do a funeral for the nearly 43,000 suicides in America each year.[1] This book is designed to assist clergy, chaplains, and other faith leaders as they develop sermons and homilies for a funeral service. Its mandate is to help those searching for inspiration even though they may feel confused or uncertain undertaking such a daunting assignment. Those who plan and lead a funeral service may enable family and friends to understand and participate intentionally in their grief process. We believe that clergy can have a significant impact on how people react to the suicide as well as provide tremendous assistance to those left behind on their journey through grief.

The Suicide Funeral is also designed for seminarians, lay ministers, funeral directors, and mental health professionals. Seminaries and theological schools of several denominations are now paying attention to the subject of suicide in courses such as biblical studies, church history, ethics, pastoral care, social concerns, and homiletics. Ministerial students may be searching for answers about how their faith intersects with this terribly misunderstood and culturally stigmatized cause of death.

In the 1960s, Edwin Shneidman initiated the scientific study of suicide, now called *Suicidology*. Sadly, funding and public recognition of the need for suicide prevention programs were largely ignored until the mid-1990s. Individuals who have lost a loved one to suicide, called *suicide survivors* or the *suicide bereaved*, have been instrumental in moving United States government policy forward and providing federal funds to prevent suicide. They have altered public understanding and treatment of suicide death in middle and high schools and higher education.

Often, addressing suicide lies in your hands as an informed spiritual leader. You will be modeling a grief journey through counseling the suicide bereaved and conducting the funeral. Your leadership will influence how the suicide bereaved are treated by other clergy, congregants, lay ministers,

1. Drapeau & McIntosh, USA Suicide 2014 Official final data

funeral directors, and others in the days, weeks, and months following the death.

Because suicide does not discriminate by race, socio-economic status, or religion, a broad range of faiths and denominations are represented in this book's sermons, services, and perspectives. Contributors include Christian and Jewish clergy; the Venerable Thubten Chodron, a Buddhist nun and author; Sheik Jamal Rahman, a Muslim Sufi and faith leader; and Bishop William Young of Memphis, Tennessee, who is widely recognized as a leader on the issue of suicide within the Black Church. While most of the sermons and perspectives were solicited for this volume, we have included reprints of texts written at a time when the subject was almost never mentioned from the pulpit except for condemnation. Reverend Doctor Norman Vincent Peale, Father Ron Rolheiser, and Father William Bausch wrote seminal works essential to a more compassionate way of thinking about suicide.

We are very pleased to include contributions from clergy and pastoral counselors who, apart from their duties as faith leaders, also wear the hat of *suicide survivor*. Each has lost a loved one to suicide and graciously contributed to this volume: Rabbi Chaya Gusfield, Rabbi Lori Klein, Reverend Doctor Karen Covey-Moore, Reverend Doctor Paul Tunkle, and Spiritual Director Anne Cronin Tyson. Their stories convey the gravitas of their personal loss, the rash of emotions and despair that guided their struggle to understand their experiences within the context of both their walks of faith and their roles as leaders.

The Language of Suicide

We have been broad in our thinking about how to characterize suicide. In most religions, there has been some development of policy (tradition) around those individuals who have died by suicide. Language often reflects the evolution of thought and church policy. In popular culture, the use of the term *commit suicide* is used by many well-intentioned who are unaware of what it conveys. Most clergy represented in this book, however, avoid using *commit* as related to the act of suicide. Most leaders in suicide prevention refrain from using *commit suicide* on the grounds that it suggests criminal or sinful activity. For centuries, many religions have considered suicide both a sin against God and a crime against the state, a heinous act that an individual deliberately chooses to do, knowing it is wrong. Leading suicidologists today hold that such language perpetuates stigma and shame, misrepresents the death, hinders efforts to prevent suicide, prevents individuals from seeking help, and thwarts broader public awareness and prevention advocacy.[2]

The website http://reportingonsuicide.org is a more recent product of the effort to make safe reporting recommendations and strategies accessible to the public and media. In 2001, leading public health, mental health, and suicide prevention organizations worked together to produce *Reporting on Suicide: Recommendations for the Media*, guidelines to help the media report on suicide with more sensitivity to language and the impact reporting may have on its audience. This significant document is an essential tool to gain a better understanding about how to better characterize suicide both in the funeral service and after. Alternative phrases, such as *took one's life* or *died by suicide* have replaced *commit* in the vernacular. This has become a crucial development for the suicide bereaved, who often feel that they share in the alienation, stigma and criminal activity inferred by the use of the word *commit*.

The editors of this book acknowledge that some religions still consider suicide a crime or a sin, and, therefore, *commit* would be an appropriate verb given their perspective. Others use *commit* because they are not aware of the suicide prevention debate; therefore, they do so out of convention and ignorance of the offense it may cause some mourners. The editors have chosen not to use the phrase *commit suicide* because we are aware of this pain and do not understand or acknowledge it as a sin.

Bibliography

Drapeau, Christopher. W., and J.L. McIntosh. *U.S.A. Suicide 2014: Official final data.* Washington, DC: American Association of Suicidology, December 22, 2015, https://dphhs.mt.gov/Portals/85/amdd/documents/Professional%20Persons/2014USSuicideData.pdf

Silverman, Morton M, MD, Alan L. Berman, PhD, Nels D. Sanddal, MS, Patrick W. O'Carroll, MD, MPH, and Thomas E. Joiner, Jr., PhD. "Rebuilding the Tower of Babel: A Revised Nomenclature for the Study of Suicide and Suicidal Behaviors. Part I: Background, Rationale, and Methodology." *Suicide and Life-Threatening Behavior* 37, No. 3, June 2007.

2. Silverman, et al, *Suicide and Life-Threatening Behavior*

A Word of Caution:
What to do When a Congregant Displays Is Suicidal

Before you find yourself counseling a suicidal person, we strongly suggest that you get some training. Talk to a mental health professional in your congregation or seek out training at a suicide prevention agency. Your community may have a Question, Persuade, and Refer (QPR) gatekeeper training course provided by The QPR Institute. The National Action Alliance Task Force for Faith Communities provides publications, webinars, and other online resources on how ministers can help. The Caring Clergy Project has online resources that can help prepare you to talk with a congregant about their suicidal ideation. The Means Matters Campaign at Harvard University teaches how to talk with a suicidal person about their access to lethal means. All of these resources are found in the appendix to this chapter.

Suicidal ideation and behavior are psychiatric emergencies which require the assistance of trained professionals. *You must act accordingly to keep the person safe.* That means, do not leave them alone for one second. Take them to a licensed mental health professional with expertise in dealing with suicidal patients or to the emergency room for further evaluation. Immediately break a confidence and reveal this encounter to the person who is closest to them or to their legal guardian.

As the Caring Clergy Project video "Responding to a Suicidal Person" indicates, it is not enough to say *pray more* when a congregant tells you through words or actions that they are suicidal. This is an indication of their need for professional help. If you suspect that they are suicidal, one technique is to simply ask them if they are thinking of killing themselves. Usually, people will be honest, for they feel relieved that someone understands their great melancholy. Ask follow-up questions, *by what means would you do this? Have you secured this instrument?* It is important to ask these questions in a nonjudgmental and caring way. All suicidal thoughts and preparatory behaviors, such as securing means to die or giving items away or writing wills, must be taken seriously.

While prayer can be an effective coping skill, it will not resolve suicidal thoughts and feelings. Therapy, medication, and support from loved ones are the best salves to heal these wounds. Yes, being suicidal might come from a spiritual crisis, but usually and generally, it is not. You do not want to minister to a suicidal person alone or dismiss him or her from your office because it is outside your competency. This is unethical, it may leave you legally exposed, and you will never be able to forgive yourself if something were to happen. You simply do not want to risk it. Get your congregant the loving help that you would want for your own child or family member.

Resources

The Caring Clergy Project: http://www.caringclergyproject.org/suicideprevention interventionresponse.html

The Means Matters Campaign: https://www.hsph.harvard.edu/means-matter/means-matter/

National Action Alliance Task Force on Faith Communities: http://actionallianceforsuicide prevention.org/faith-communities. Also see www.Faith-Hope-Life.org, a product of the National Action Alliance and a campaign to encourage all faith communities to embrace suicide prevention (through prevention and postvention).

National Suicide Prevention Lifeline is a toll-free and confidential national suicide prevention hotline and can be accessed 24/7:1–800-273–8255 (TALK).

The QPR Institute: Question, Persuade and Refer: https://www.qprinstitute.com/.

Acknowledgments

This book would not have been possible had it not been for the vision of Dr. James T. Clemons. His untimely death during the writing of this book left a void. His spiritual presence was a continual source of inspiration behind this book and the alliance between the authors and contributors. After Jim's death, Melinda floundered to finalize this book, ultimately shelving the project, until she was introduced to Rabbi Dan Roberts by her friend and Suicidology colleague, Dr. Julie Cerel. Melinda acknowledges that this book would not have been possible had it not been for both Jim and Dan's presence, both men of God, both touched profoundly by suicide. Humans interceded and acted, but, clearly, God had His hand in it.

The authors are deeply appreciative to Dr. David Litts, who formerly headed the Air Force's model suicide prevention program and is now an expert on public communications in support of suicide prevention. His efforts to reduce prejudice and discrimination that prevent many people from seeking and receiving effective mental health treatment is also focused on statements made about and by faith communities. He serves in leadership on the National Action Alliance's Faith Communities Task Force and graciously vetted our sermons for safe messaging to ensure their effectiveness and security.

This book simply could not have been realized had it not been for all of the authors and contributors to this book. We are deeply grateful for their written work and their ongoing service to people in their faith communities, congregations, and sanghas. Anne Cronin Tyson and Kristen Spexarth were especially helpful in making connections and supporting the editors during the process of constructing the various parts of the book.

Dominican priest, scholar, and contributor Father John Corbett is to be acknowledged for his ongoing support and friendship to both Jim and Melinda during the early days of the book. As a former student of Jim's and a spiritual mentor to Melinda, his model of managing the messy emotional aftermath of a suicide and how to conduct oneself as clergy through the mourning rituals were deeply appreciated.

Audrey Katzman was our tireless editor and earned our undying gratitude for her work on this project, invaluable suggestions, and humor that buoyed our own mood throughout the process. Thanks also go to David Flexer for completing the final editing.

A debt of gratitude is due to Dr. Frank Campbell, the inveterate designer of the Active Postvention model and unstoppable advocate for suicide postvention through Local Outreach to Suicide Support (LOSS) teams throughout the world. Dr. Campbell has been a source of moral support as well as source of content for this book. His mastery of metaphor and contribution to chapter six is greatly appreciated. Eastern Kentucky University Clinical Psychology doctoral student Ms. Rebecca Aghamiri also contributed significantly to this chapter, and the editors are grateful for her contribution.

Chapter One

Addressing Suicide and Its Aftermath

Melinda Moore, PhD

Suicide, perhaps more than any other cause of death, challenges our ways of thinking about the person who has died and our relationship to them. Inevitably, existential and religious questions arise among the surviving loved ones, the *suicide bereaved*, as they struggle with their relationships to God and with the upheaval of their comfort zones. Ministers, priests, rabbis, and other faith leaders who conduct suicide funerals are in a unique position to help. Yet, like other professionals who interact with the suicide bereaved, such as medical and behavioral health providers, clergy seldom receive training to address suicide within their community or their professional setting. According to the National Action Alliance's Faith Communities Task Force,[1] a survey of clergy indicated that suicide-related course work is seldom offered in seminaries, and suicide may only be addressed by clergy within their own faith community at a moment when they are expected to demonstrate leadership. This is really too late. The dearth of training forces clergy and seminarians to fall back on their own opinions and life experiences. Assumptions may color their understanding of suicide and may impair their ability to adequately minister to those who are suicidal. They will also impact the health and wellbeing of the suicide bereaved.

1. The National Action Alliance, "The Role of Faith Communities in Suicide Prevention."

1

The Science of Suicide Exposure

Within the last twenty years, the science around why people become suicidal, how to intervene with a suicidal individual, and the serious consequences of a suicide on a community or on the suicide bereaved has evolved quickly. Part of that rapid growth has been the development of "best" practices for safe messaging concerning suicide in media broadcasts and/or a public speech, such as a funeral homily or sermon. Guides to public messaging about suicide are available on websites such as http://reportingonsuicide. org/. Additionally, the National Action Alliance's Faith Task Force website (www.faith-hope-life.org) is tailored to the needs of faith communities and clergy. National efforts to understand and respond to the needs of those impacted by suicide are also beautifully covered in the document *Responding to Grief, Trauma, and Distress After a Suicide: U.S. National Guidelines*.[2]

Through a eulogy, clergy are uniquely positioned to demonstrate leadership by guiding family members, parishioners, and others to compassionately react to a suicide death. Best practices are free of details that may romanticize or demonize the death and do not mislead with opinions that are not consistent with science or much agreed-upon Church and other faith community policies. Such leadership begins in the chaotic time immediately after the suicide when loved ones are struggling with the trauma and continues through the funeral service and the aftermath, which continues for years.

Several factors make this book especially timely. Each year, more than 800,000 people die internationally by suicide,[3] and the World Health Organization declared that suicide must be made a public health priority worldwide. In the United States, suicide is the tenth leading cause of death with 42,773 Americans dying by suicide in 2014,[4] the last year for which we have data. This number is up from 41,149 in 2013.[5] Suicide continues to be the second leading cause of death among young Americans aged fifteen to thirty-four. Since 2010, there has been a spike among Americans in the age category from thirty-five to sixty-four. Celebrities such as Robin Williams fit within this demographic and represent the tragedy of such loss both

2. The National Action Alliance, "Responding to Grief, Trauma, and Distress After a Suicide: U.S. National Guidelines."

3. World Health Organization, *Preventing Suicide: A Global Imperative*.

4. Centers for Disease Control and Prevention, "Injury Prevention and Control, Data and Statistics (WISQARS)."

5. American Association of Suicidology, U.S.A. Suicide 2013: Official Final Data.

privately and as a cultural icon. Suicide has been increasing among women (white non-Hispanic and Hispanic women in particular) and among men (white non-Hispanic men only). The largest increase is among white men from 20.4 per 100,000 in 2000 to 27.6 per 100,000 in 2014. Out of every 100,000 men in 2014, seven more were dying by suicide compared with fifteen years earlier. Among white women, there was also a steady increase from 4.9 to 7.9 per 100,000. Out of every 100,000 women in 2014, three more were dying by suicide compared with 2000. But the percentage increase (about 60 percent) was larger for women than for men. Suicide has always been a problem among older Americans, especially among men eighty-five years of age and older, who have a suicide rate four times the average rate of most Americans.[6]

Military personnel, both active and retired, are not immune. Since September 11, 2001, more than 3,000 service members have died by suicide.[7] In 2012 and 2013, suicide was the leading cause of death for service members. It is reported that 20 percent of all U.S. suicide deaths are represented by veterans, even though less than 1 percent of the US population has served in the most recent conflicts. The Veterans Affairs Administration has estimated that their often-touted figure of twenty-two veterans dying by suicide every day is conservative. The number is likely much higher, though difficult to calculate.[8]

Suicide presents huge barriers for the loved ones and community members left behind. Though now considered flawed, earlier research demonstrated that 7 percent of all Americans surveyed were exposed to a suicide death, and 1 percent knew someone well who died by suicide and felt emotionally impacted from that death.[9] In the suicidology community, the number of individuals who are impacted by a suicide death has historically been reported as six—an erroneous claim made by Dr. Edwin Shneidman, founder of the study of suicide, but not based on empirical evidence. Dr. Julie Cerel at the University of Kentucky has dedicated much of her professional career to researching the effects of suicide exposure. Dr. Cerel and her research team at the University of Kentucky, as well as my research team at Eastern Kentucky University, are pioneering ways of

6. Centers for Disease Control and Prevention, "Injury Prevention and Control, Data and Statistics (WISQARS)."

7. USA Today, "Suicide Surpassed War as the Military's Leading Cause of Death."

8. Department of Veteran's Affairs, "Suicide Data Report, 2012."

9. Crosby and Sacks, "Exposure to Suicide," 321–328

better understanding the number of people impacted and the effects of suicide on those left behind. The results are staggering so far, and they suggest that previous and erroneously calculated numbers are much higher. Cerel's Twitter campaign, #NOT6, highlights the gravity of this impact. For every suicide death, there may be as many as 135 people who knew the person and are affected by their suicide.

More recently, Cerel and colleagues found that nearly half of all individuals in several studies knew someone who died by suicide.[10] However, simply knowing someone who died by suicide does not necessarily signal significant emotional impact. Suicide impact may actually exist on a continuum (see Figure 1) from suicide exposure to suicide bereaved, short and long-term.[11] The depth of impact is related to the bereaved's perception of "emotional" closeness to the decedent—not necessarily being biologically connected or geographically close. This could be anyone from a college roommate, a neighbor, a work colleague, a fellow parishioner, etc. More problematic is the finding that suicide bereaved individuals with higher feelings of closeness to the deceased are at elevated risk for serious mental health outcomes, such as depression and anxiety, as well as increased risk of suicidal ideation[12, 13] and suicide attempts.[14] Bereavement from suicide has been long been associated with psychiatric disorders (see Figure 2) such as Post Traumatic Stress Disorder and Prolonged Grief Disorder.[1516] Addressing the mental health needs of the suicide bereaved is one of the best suicide prevention measures.

10. Cerel et al, "Suicide Exposure in the Community."
11. Cerel et al, "The Continuum of Survivorship."
12. Cerel, "We Are All Connected in Suicidology."
13. Cerel et al, "Suicide Exposure in the Community."
14. Pitman et al, "Bereavement by Suicide as a Risk Factor for Suicide Attempt."
15. Mitchell et al, "Complicated Grief in Survivors of Suicide"
16. Latham and Prigerson, "Suicidality and Bereavement."

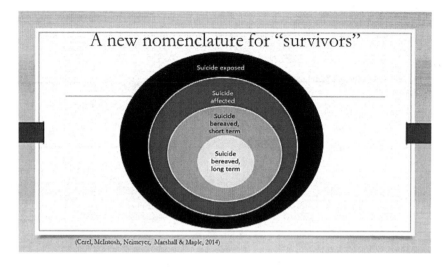

Figure 1

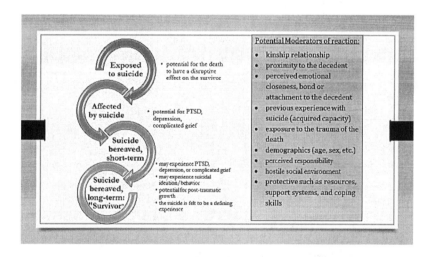

Figure 2 (Cerel, McIntosh, Neimeyer, Marshall & Maple, 2014)

Postvention as Prevention

What complicates grieving for many suicide bereaved is stigma. Popular American culture is rife with stigma around suicide, including blaming

5

loved ones for the suicide death.[17] Depending upon the individual personalities and attitudes toward suicide by the suicide bereaved and their network, social support may frequently be different and more difficult.[18] The loss of social support due to the stigmatized nature of suicide, which may bleed over onto the bereaved family members, may account for both the social isolation and withdrawal from social interaction and comfort. There is considerable evidence that suicide bereaved feel more isolated and stigmatized than other mourners.[19] Suicide bereaved individuals may also pre-emptively "self-stigmatize" and reject the awkward offerings of help and support from individuals who genuinely wish to help but are uncomfortable and uncertain about how to proceed. Instead, the bereaved perceive their discomfort and uncertainty as rejection. Bereaved individuals may also mirror negative cultural attitudes toward suicide, which then causes them to assume that others are judging them. Either approach may deprive the suicide bereaved of much needed support and understanding from their social network.[20] Their internalized feelings of cultural stigma around suicide may also interfere with their willingness to seek help,[21] thus leaving them further at risk for depression, anxiety, suicidal ideation, and suicide attempt with no hope of a professional identifying it and providing them with lifesaving treatment.

Efforts to get the suicide bereaved into some form of assistance has been forwarded by innovations in "suicide postvention" or interventions for those exposed to and impacted by suicide. Dr. Frank Campbell pioneered the Active Postvention Model,[22] a model of support for suicide bereaved on the location of the actual suicide, called Local Outreach to Suicide Support (LOSS) Teams. Working with law enforcement and county coroners, LOSS Teams, who are specifically trained by Dr. Campbell and other suicide postvention experts, are a first response resource for the purpose of reducing the length of time between the death and finding help for the newly bereaved. The Active Postvention Model has reduced the length of time that a suicide bereaved is referred and seeks help to less than sixty days. Prior to this model, the average time was four and a half years.[23] LOSS Teams now exist across the United

---

17. Harwood, et al, "The Grief Experiences and Needs of Bereaved Relatives and Friends."

18. Jordan, "Is Suicide Bereavement Different?"

19. Mitchell et al, "The Use of Narrative Data."

20. Jordan, "Is Suicide Bereavement Different?"

21. Pitman et al, "Bereavement by Suicide as a Risk Factor."

22. Campbell, "Changing the Legacy of Suicide."

23. Ibid.

States and internationally and act as models of what can be created within a faith community when a suicide death occurs. Lay ministers and faith leaders may be activated to compassionately and nonjudgmentally appear on the site of the suicide to provide information and resources, as well as show love and support to the newly bereaved. What better way to demonstrate the love of God in those moments of intense pain and isolation.

Clergy's Leadership Roles

Clergy are in a unique position to lead when it comes to how we think about suicide. The vocabulary we use and our treatment of individuals who may be impacted and at risk for suicide themselves can have tremendous influence. Faith leaders are true first responders, similar to emergency medical personnel who roll up on a tragedy and begin triage. Clergy become trusted messengers of hope, assuring the bereaved that the sun will come up another day and that reconciliation is possible. Each death presents challenges and opportunities, and no two suicide funerals are alike. One way of addressing the individuality of the deceased and the mourners can be through "experimental restorying." This approach enables survivors of loss, through telling the story of the person's full life, to work through problems seen and unseen or even denied. This technique emerges from narrative therapy whereby an individual uses a story or multiple stories from their life to enrich their own life narrative, heightening emotional awareness and meaning.[24] The hearer gathers stories, analyzes them for key elements such as time, place, or plot, and collaboratively rewrites the story to place it in a sequence that makes sense for the person telling the story.

Clergy are able to adopt this approach in working with stories of the Bible as they minister to the needs of the suicide bereaved. Using biblical or other religious stories as models of wrestling with faith struggles, the bereaved are able to openly process their questioning as well as discomfort around questioning tenants of their faith. Clinical Psychologists Dr. Kalman J. Kaplan and Dr. Paul Cantz are pioneering the integration of Greek and biblical narratives to use within the context of psychotherapy as an alternative to or in partnership with the traditional clinical approach. A recently co-authored book, *Biblical Psychotherapy: Reclaiming Scriptural Narratives for Positive Psychology and Suicide Prevention*, is a resource for clergy and mental health professionals alike. Drs. Kaplan and Cantz train psychologists, social

24. White, *Maps of Narrative Practice*.

7

workers, pastoral counselors, and chaplains in this approach through an on-line course titled "A Biblical Approach to Mental Health" at the University of Illinois at Chicago's College of Medicine in conjunction with Spertus Institute of Jewish Learning and Leadership. By teaching clinicians and religious counselors to artfully open up religious narratives for self-exploration and understanding, they are offering a broader perspective on issues that may not be adequately addressed in more traditional mental health counseling. For the suicide bereaved, this approach may help clinicians to more deeply explore intrusive and unwelcome thoughts that frequently accompany the experience of a suicide death.

What Does The Bible Say About Suicide and What Do We Need To Say?

While suicide is not specifically condemned in Jewish and Christian scriptures, the Church for centuries condemned those who took their lives, denying funeral services and refusing last rites and burial in consecrated cemeteries. In early Christian writings, known as the Apostolic Fathers (CE 96 to 150), there was no explicit condemnation of suicide. In fact, the writings of Ignatius and the account of Polycarp's martyrdom, as well as other Christian martyrs, characterized self-chosen death for pious reasons as acceptable and, at times, an honoured Judeo-Christian behavior.[25] It was not until the time of Augustine in the fourth century that the position set forth against suicide was widely adopted. Augustine's view that the Sixth Commandment, Thou Shalt Not Murder, was interpreted as a strict prohibition against suicide and later reinforced by Thomas Aquinas, Martin Luther, John Wesley, and other theologians.[26]

Culture has significantly influenced the Church's position on suicide. Variations in biblical interpretation are due partly to constant social forces influencing the Church.[27] Today, an increasing number of faith-based communities are re-examining their positions in light of sociological and psychological studies and advances in medicine and psychiatry. Yet, superstition, the persistence of stigma, and misunderstanding of religious teachings still profoundly affect the lives of many touched by suicide.

25. Clemons, *What Does the Bible Say About Suicide?*

26. Clemons, *Sermons on Suicide*

27. Clemons, *What Does the Bible Say About Suicide?*

Counseling by clergy in the aftermath of suicide may predict in part the trajectory of grief experienced by family and friends. Openly exhibiting your emotions, should the story touch you, should not be withheld. Listening carefully to their grief, their confusion, and their worry that their relationship with God has been inalterably disrupted because of this loss is a *sine qua non*. This latter concern may be a critical step in ministering to their spiritual needs, for many feel that they are wearing a *scarlet letter*—a mark of shame that everyone sees or knows about. The inability to integrate this loss into their understanding of a compassionate God, or a sense of justice in the world, is often an intellectual and spiritual disconnect that many suicide bereaved confront in their lonely walk into the unknown abyss of the future. We can help them to find the rope bridge downstream that will carry them over this depth. For those who had no faith or relationship with God before, we can assist them through this minefield and perhaps help them in a spiritual quest.

After my husband Conor's suicide, I recall sitting with a compassionate stranger, Father Bill Maroon, a priest to whom I had been referred by one of his parishioners in Columbus, Ohio. I was a new Catholic, having converted and entered the church the year before my husband's suicide. I was uncertain how to make sense of my new faith in the context of the most painful, spiritual event of my life. Other clergy with whom I had come in contact had been unable to answer my questions as to how to assimilate this experience into my journey of faith. Father Maroon sat and cried with me, recounting—really re-teaching in a profound way—stories of Job's coping with enormous grief and his questions about where God was in the midst of suffering. In that moment of intense pain, I was given permission to question, like Job, God's whereabouts, to sink deeply into my disappointment and grief, to question, and to once again rejoin God in a loving embrace. Through Father Maroon's fearless compassion and restorying of Job, I was profoundly taught how close our modern-day experiences are to those in the Bible and how real God's mercy is for us and our loved ones. I will never forget this godly man and how healing his ministry of aftercare was for me and how it allowed me to begin the task of reshaping my grief.

Because Conor was Irish and came to the United States to study at The Ohio State University, I wanted to participate in an Irish tradition of the "Month's Mind Mass," a mass that occurs one month after death as a way of celebrating the deceased's life of faith and commending them to the Lord. I thought this would be an opportunity to invite his friends and colleagues at

Ohio State to participate in a memorial ceremony because they were unable to attend his funeral and burial in Ireland. I was in unchartered territory and was uncertain how the priest would handle the disposition of Conor's soul during the mass. I was certain that his soul was with God, but my own friends' and family's reaction to his suicide, not to mention my community newspaper's and my work colleagues' apparent horror, communicated something different. Even a local priest, a friend of Conor's father, told me that he was not *certain of the disposition of Conor's soul*, in response to my question about my own walk of faith. It was as if Conor's act of self-destruction obfuscated the ministering to my own need for clarity about how to understand his death. It was clear that people who surrounded me weren't sure about his soul. I suspected they weren't certain about my soul, and this made the experience of celebrating his life of faith in a Catholic Church—much less *commending him to the Lord*—uncomfortable.

I was also nervous because I knew the priests of St. Patrick's Church, a church supported by the Dominican Order, were a more traditional, conservative order, especially Father Stephen Hayes, the American-born, Gaelic-speaking lawyer/priest who was conducting this mass. I was nervous but obedient, knowing that Fr. Hayes would handle it the appropriate way, even if it caused pain and discomfort in my own heart. When Father Hayes entered the church and began the service reverently, not gratuitously or pandering to our pain, asserting that Conor's soul was with God by virtue of his baptism, all questions were vanquished, all doubt erased, and all misrepresented Church policy redirected. There seemed to be a sigh of relief among the attendees, as if they, too, feared condemnation. Father Hayes showed leadership, compassion, and a profound understanding in his very first utterance. I will never forget the moment and how it provided enormous comfort in my time of greatest pain and buoyed my own faith practice, even all these years later.

Bibliography

Campbell, Frank R. "Changing the Legacy of Suicide." *Suicide and Life Threatening Behavior* 27, no. 4 (Winter 1997).

Centers for Disease Control. "Injury Prevention and Control, Data and Statistics (WISQARS)." Downloaded 1–10-2016 from http://www.cdc.gov/injury/wisqars/index.html.

Cerel, Julie. "We Are All Connected in Suicidology: The Continuum of *Survivorship*." Lecture, American Association of Suicidology Annual Conference, Atlanta, GA, April 2015.

————, John L. McIntosh, Robert A. Neimeyer, Myfanwy Maple, and Doreen Marshall. "The Continuum of "Survivorship": Definitional Issues in the Aftermath of Suicide." *Suicide and Life-Threatening Behavior* 44, no. 6 (2014): 591–600.

————, Myfanwy Maple, Judy Van De Venne, Melinda Moore, Chris Flaherty, and Margaret Brown. "Exposure to Suicide in the Community: Prevalence and Correlates in One U.S. State." *Public Health Report* 131, no. 1 (January/February 2016): 100–107.

Clemons, James. *Sermons on Suicide.* Louisville: Westminster/John Knox Press, 1989.

————. *What Does the Bible Say About Suicide?* Minneapolis: Fortress Press, 1990.

Crosby, Alex E., and Jeffrey J. Sacks. "Exposure to Suicide: Incidence and Association with Suicidal Ideation and Behavior: United States, 1994." *Suicide and Life-Threatening Behavior* 32, no. 3 (2002): 321–328.

Department of Veterans Affairs. "Suicide Data Report, 2012." http://www.va.gov/opa/docs/suicide-data-report-2012-final.pdf

Harwood, Daniel, Keith Hawton, Tony Hope, and Robin Jacoby. "The Grief Experiences and Needs of Bereaved Relatives and Friends of Older People Dying through Suicide: A Descriptive and Case-control Study." *Journal of Affective Disorders* 72, no. 2 (2002): 185–194.

Jordan, John R. "Is Suicide Bereavement Different? A Reassessment of the Literature." *Suicide and Life-Threatening Behavior* 31, no. 1 (2001): 91–102. doi.org/10.1521/suli.31.1.91.21310

Latham, Amy E., and Holly G. Prigerson. "Suicidality and Bereavement: Complicated Grief as Psychiatric Disorder Presenting Greatest Risk for Suicidality." *Suicide and Life-Threatening Behavior* 34, no. 4 (2004): 350–362. doi.org/10.1521/suli.34.4.350.53737

Mitchell, Ann M., Deborah Dysart Gale, Linda Garand, and Susan Wesner. "The Use of Narrative Data to Inform the Psychotherapeutic Group Process with Suicide Survivors." *Issues in Mental Health Nursing* 24, no. 1 (2003): 91–106. doi.org/10.1080/01612840305308

————, Yookyung Kim, Holly G. Prigerson, and Marykay Mortimer-Stephens. "Complicated Grief in Survivors of Suicide." *Crisis* 25, no. 1 (2004): 12–18. doi:10.1027/0227-5910.25.1.12

National Action Alliance. "The Role of Faith Communities in Suicide Prevention," Webinar, December 3, 2015, https://edc.adobeconnect.com/_a1002235226/p192idot1n3/

————. "Responding to Grief, Trauma, and Distress After a Suicide: U.S. National Guidelines." http://actionallianceforsuicideprevention.org/sites/actionallianceforsuicideprevention.org/files/NationalGuidelines.pdf

Pitman, Alexandra L., David P J Osborn, Khadija Rantell, and Michael B. King. "Bereavement by Suicide as a Risk Factor for Suicide Attempt: A Cross-sectional National UK-wide Study of 3432 Young Bereaved Adults." *BMJ Open* 6, no. 1 (2016). doi:10.1136/bmjopen-2015-009948

USA Today. "Suicide Surpassed War as the Military's Leading Cause of Death." http://www.usatoday.com/story/nation/2014/10/31/suicide-deaths-us-military-war-study/18261185/

White, Michael. *Maps of Narrative Practice.* New York: WW Norton & Company, 2007.

World Health Organization. *Preventing Suicide: A Global Imperative,* Luxembourg: World Health Organization, 2014.

Chapter Two

Preparing a Eulogy or Memorial Service for One Who Died by Suicide
Some Thoughts

Rabbi Daniel A. Roberts, DD, DMin, FT

As a clergyperson, you well know that the next phone call could be one that directs you to the very reason you chose this meaningful world: to be available at another's time of need. From past experience, you are aware that some funerals are *easy*—when a person was elderly and lived a full life, and the death was expected. Some are more difficult—when the death was unexpected, sudden, and the deceased was young. The most difficult funeral of all will be when a person has ended her/his own life. No experience in your repertoire is equivalent to dealing with a death through suicide.

This death not only affects the bereaved family but goes beyond in concentric circles to friends, colleagues, and even to you. It zaps the survivors' emotional strength and leaves many lingering *why* questions. Why did this person elect to die? Why did I miss the signs? Why could I have not prevented it? Why did a supposedly caring God allow this to happen? Why? *Why?* Unlike a natural death, guilt and blame seem to overwhelm the mourners. They seem to be trapped in the moment of death, trying to figure out what the person was experiencing or how they could have prevented it. Family and friends engage in magical thinking. *I could have prevented this death; I should have known this was going to happen.* It is a time of shock, trauma, and chaos, a time of should'ves, could'ves, would'ves.

As a forewarning, this funeral will consume your energy and leave its mark on you for years to come. The pain of the mourners is enormous and overwhelming, and you have stepped into a quagmire. It would be wise to alert your mate and your family that this is going to be a tough time, and you might not be emotionally available for a while. Despite these caveats, this may be one of the most meaningful moments in your career and one in which you can have great impact. You will not only be a comfort to family and friends, you can help them come to terms with what appears to be a senseless moment. Moreover, you have the potential to prevent contagion. Your words can prevent another human being from contemplating suicide as a solution to their darkened world. It is a powerful moment in your career, in your life.

And So the Adventure Begins

Where to Meet the Family:

It is the suggestion of this author that you meet the family on their home turf, where they are most comfortable and feel secure. When you enter that space, you must check your curiosity at the doorstep. Like everyone else, you would love to know all the details, what happened and when and how. This is a natural response. However, put that urge aside; probing is not your job. The family has had enough of that from the police and others. The authorities may suspect their involvement in the death and may not be treating them sensitively. If you are *silent*, you will learn all the details along the way. You are there to comfort, to bring some order in a time of crisis. They are at a loss, not knowing what to do next, and your role is to assist them in getting through the next few hellish days as they make new order in their lives.

The one unique aspect of being a clergyperson is that when you approach this family, even if they have never met you, you are immediately taken in as a family member. From their past experiences, from sermons of comfort they have heard, from images of the ideal clergy, they believe that *you* have the potential to make order of chaos and will bring some solace to them. Allowing the family to talk, to reminisce, to show pictures, and to recall moments of joy helps them to make some sense of this unfathomable experience. They will recognize that you are their advocate and can perhaps comprehend the pain they are enduring. You may be able to lead them on a path of understanding what happened and to lie down again in "green pastures."

Leave your theology on the doorstep:

Your role is to *listen*. Listen to the story; listen to the beautiful moments of a life cut short; listen to sad souls who were not prepared for a sudden death and now have to figure out how to live without their loved one. You must listen to people who are in shock and trauma and let them talk. It is therapeutic. Ask questions only to fill in gaps where you do not understand the sequence and to lead them into the story of their loved one and help them make sense of the death. Then, perhaps, you can help them bring some order to their lives.

At some point in the dialogue, they will challenge you. Since they see you as God's representative, they will cry out, *why did God let this happen?* Do not fall into the trap of thinking that they seek theological answers; the family has neither the patience nor the inclination to hear them. They are venting their anger; they do not want theology. Your role is to comfort, not defend God. If God cannot deal with our anger at moments like this, then, indeed, God should have prevented it. In my concept, God has much broader shoulders and does not reject people who question *why*. This is not the time to blame anyone—even the one who died by suicide should not be blamed for the pain they have caused. Nor is this the time for condemnation, even "lite" condemnation. If you feel this way about one who dies by suicide, then your participation would do a disservice to the family, so recuse yourself and allow someone else to do the funeral. Don't pretend that you are what you are not. At this time, the family needs comfort, compassion, care, and love.

Listen:

Hear the story and recognize that it will be disjointed. The picture of the deceased's life will seem like a puzzle. Threads and themes will emerge, but do not force the family to follow them. What they need is to tell the story, so let them ramble. Do not impose a time limit on your meetings, and be open to listening as long as it takes. This visit will take much longer than an ordinary condolence call because there is a need to listen to *everyone* involved. Try to include everyone that is touched by this death, giving each an opportunity to talk and emote. For other funerals, you might not include the grandparents, siblings, and friends in the conversation, but in this case, you must! Everyone will be affected differently and will be in shock and hurting. Give them time to tell—and perhaps re-tell—their stories, as talking is the best therapy. Use open-ended questions and prompts. Tell me about _____. Give me a couple of words that best describes _____. Tell me one value that best summarizes _____'s life. Describe a time when _____ particularly touched your life. This is time well invested. Later, when you sit down to write the eulogy, it will somehow all fit together.

If this is the death of a young person, work particularly hard to make sure that contagion does not take place. Friends who may believe that choosing suicide is a way to get attention or escape their problems may be deterred by your words. You have the ability to encourage them to choose life instead of a premature death. No matter the age of the deceased, help the family and friends develop ways to constructively memorialize the deceased. You must also lead them to find ways to deal with their loss.

Yes, you can speak:

Your words need to be words of comfort. Although all of this is a mystery, speak of God being with them in the journey ahead. Talk about the difficult moments ahead and remind the survivors that many happy moments ahead will ease the pain. You must be frank with them that grief is a journey that never ends; one just learns to deal with painful moments. Time will soften the grief, but it will not heal it. With suicide, one is left with a cognitive scar that hurts forever, rather like having a limb amputated. The survivors will never be the same and will need to relearn how to manage life. You can inform mourners of the difficulties ahead in the first year, like celebrating the first family event without their loved one and facing the person's birthday without them. It is important to reassure them that there will be moments of joy again in the future. A wonderful book to suggest they read is *The Long Shadow of Grief* by Harold Ivan Smith.

You can question:

This is a time for questions about the memorial service or funeral. What thoughts do the family and friends have about the service? Should certain people be invited to speak? Would certain music bring comfort? Is there a special poem, reading, or liturgy that reflects the deceased?

Help the mourners discuss their feelings about revealing that this was a suicide. Suicide—and the phrase *died by suicide*—is the elephant in the room. You might point out that ignoring or hiding this will only cause anxiety for others, who will tiptoe around the subject. They will be uncomfortable addressing the reality of suicide and afraid to talk to the mourners. Consequently, you and the mourners will also be afraid of *slipping up* as you try to keep the suicide a "secret." However, you do need to explore the family's feelings about mentioning suicide. The last thing you want is for their anger to shift to you because they intended that you keep the suicide a secret. They will seek your guidance about sharing the secret, so spend some heartfelt moments considering how you would handle this if it were your child or relative. Reassure the family that you will handle this subject gently and not focus on the manner of death.

The Eulogy

Complications of Writing a Eulogy:

The first word is always the hardest, but this will be complicated by the fact that, in this type of eulogy, you need to choose your words with great care. Unlike other funerals, you need to deliberate on *how* to speak about the suicide. You do not want to glorify suicide nor make the family feel any more responsible for the death than they already do. We encourage you to weigh every word. In our sample eulogies, we have vetted words to prevent a contagion effect or the idealization of death. You should also be concerned about making Heaven such an ideal place that a bereaved mourner might desire to get there sooner rather than later. In chapter 7, we give you some pegs on which to hang the beginning or the end of a eulogy and illustrative themes with which you can string the elements of a person's life together.

The tone of your voice will be as important as the words you speak. This is the time for your loving, compassionate voice and not a voice with harsh undertones. In the eulogy itself, longer is not better. George Burns once said, *the secret of a good sermon is to have a good beginning and a good ending—and to have the two as close together as possible.* And so it is here. This is not the time to defend God, as some eulogies tend to do. Instead, try to show the deceased as a real person who had love and concern for others, who wrestled with depression, and who saw suicide as the only answer to the pain they endured. This person also gave a piece of their soul to others. In a sense, this eulogy is like one for someone who died suddenly in a car accident or by a heart attack. For those who died from other causes, you would be effusive and complimentary. Just because this person died by their own hand, you should not short change the moments of beauty in their life. Remember, too, that the funeral is not for the one who died but for the bereaved. In their grief and anguish, they must be comforted and allowed to mourn. They will need to call upon their resiliency to crawl through the next days and months of their lives. Your words can be of great assistance. They will be forever indebted to you and walk away from the moment with compliments for how you handled the situation.

It is Not Over When the Eulogy is Completed

Continued Care:

The beauty of being a clergyperson is that people regard you as a member of the family, and they sense that your suggestions and instructions come from your heart and are meant to help not harm. This gives you the advantage of being able to share knowledge that can assist them in dealing with the loss. Their friends mean well but often give foolish advice, like, *you need to get over this. Go back to work and take your mind off of it. Go on a vacation. You don't need professional help, just decide that you can get through this.* As a clergyperson, you know better. Unlike other losses, this death will require additional follow-up. The family will need ongoing care and will need to talk their way through their grief. Therefore, sometime after the funeral, you need to visit with the family and suggest resources in the community for survivors of suicide. Remind them of the up and down journey of bereavement. Discuss ways to memorialize their loved one, as memorialization helps them feel that they can move this death beyond a tragedy. It also gives continued meaning to the bereaved.

Continued Care for Yourself:

Life does not just go on for you even though a thousand things are begging for your attention and you feel obligated to handle them. You have changed. At this funeral, more than any other, you will confront your existential self. It is not uncommon to wonder about suicide yourself, wonder what the world would be without you, and imagine the world to come. It may be just a fleeting thought, but it is there. You might ask yourself, if told you had a terminal illness, would you choose to end your life so as to avoid the pain?

Also, you are spent emotionally; you're exhausted. You need to take time out.

You will be a more effective minister, colleague, partner, parent, or grandparent if you not only take time to process this death, but also care for yourself physically and emotionally. It may be helpful to find a social worker, psychologist, or a good friend who will just listen to what you went through. You won't need advice; you will need love and compassion. Engage in some exercise and do something enjoyable.

Bibliography

Craig, Mary Robin. "Care for Suicide Survivors." The Huffington Post. June 12, 2013. http://www.huffingtonpost.com/rev-mary-robin-craig/care-for-suicide-survivors_b_3064300.html.

Parachin, Victor M. "Left Behind: Ministering to Survivors After a Suicide." Enrichment Journal. Summer 2010. http://enrichmentjournal.ag.org/201003/ejonline_201003_left_behind.cfm.

Smith, Harold Ivan. A Long Shadowed Grief: Suicide and its Aftermath. Cambridge: Cowley Publications, 2006.

Chapter Three

Sample Eulogies

∽

The Civil Funeral Ceremony

ANN M. DAVIES

Caring for the funeral needs of those bereaved by suicide in the UK of no specific religious persuasion, a model service included.

Introduction

The number of people in Great Britain who participate in formal religious worship within the Anglican, Roman Catholic Communion, and other Christian denominations, such as Methodist and Baptists, is decreasing year on year. In a census encompassing 7,000 participants conducted by the Tearfund in 2007, the following statement appeared in the resulting report:

> Two thirds of UK adults (66 percent) or 32.2 million people have no connection with church at present, (nor with another religion). These people are evenly divided between those who have been in the past but have since left (16 million) and those who have never been in their lives (16.2 million) . . . Most of them—29.3 million

are unreceptive and closed to attending church; churchgoing is simply not on their agenda.[1]

The cumulative effect of this secularization is that, among the public at large, there is disregard for formalized religion on the one hand, and on the other hand, a growing trend towards people describing themselves as "spiritual."[2]

Developing from these trends is the rejection of some long held liturgical funeral rites and a growing demand for a funeral service in keeping with the deceased's beliefs and those of the bereaved. Out of this social phenomenon has emerged the role of the Civil Funeral Celebrant. The celebrant undergoes a formal training period to learn:

- The principles of gathering and organizing material that will form the funeral ceremony

- How to interview the bereaved with sensitivity and collect the information that will form the tribute

- The art of tribute writing

- Understanding the funeral industry in terms of the appropriation of the roles of funeral directors, crematoria and burial ground staff, the funeral celebrant

- Public speaking and delivery in the setting of the crematoria chapel

- Understanding of and familiarity with the Dead Citizens Charter[3]

As a practicing Roman Catholic and someone who has spent forty years in religious life, I find the beauty of the Roman Catholic Funeral Mass a rich and comforting ritual for the bereaved. At the time I experienced a suicide bereavement of a close companion in religious life, it was in the reception of her body into church the night before and the accompanying service; the concelebrated Mass the following day, and the dignified prayers and rites at the crematorium that sustained me at this time of deep shock and distress.

However, it is my experience that such comfort from these ceremonies arises not from the ceremony itself but rather when that liturgy represents

1. Ashworth, *Churchgoing in the UK: A Research Report from Tearfund on Church Attendance in the UK*, 5

2. Barley, *Christian Roots, Contemporary Spirituality*, 7

3. Young, "Dead Citizen's Charter."

the belief of those participating in it, and the rites are delivered with sensitivity and an accompanying depth of spirituality on the part of the celebrant. When either one of those two factors are absent, the funeral rite is less meaningful and less helpful in dealing with the death of someone very close and, in particular, a suicide bereavement. If both elements are absent, then the funeral rite can be painful, meaningless, and increase the distress already present as a result of a suicide death. The worst instance of the lack of both these elements was the case of a mother who lost her son to suicide. She was not a church-goer but turned for support to her local Anglican vicar. The minister took no effort in involving the mother and immediate family in the preparation of the funeral service or in explaining the meaning of the funeral rite. Therefore, the family found neither comfort nor the presence of God in the service. In addition, the minister expressed his disapproval of the mother's choice of cremation and declared he would not be able to handle the ashes of her son when the time came for them to be scattered, since the boy had taken his own life.

For much of my religious life, I have been immersed in the secular world, mixing, working, and socializing with people who have no religious belief. During that time, I have experienced from many non-religious people or non-church-goers faith in God either in their belief of a personal God or a power greater than themselves, hope in the future both in this life and an afterlife, and the expression of love between individuals and among communities of people. As well as my work in education and administration, I have over the years provided retreats for the bereaved and long before my own bereavement had always taken an active interest in care for the bereaved. It is against that background of living and working in a secular world along with my interest in the care of the bereaved that God guided me to the work of being a Funeral Celebrant. Let it be said here that each Civil Celebrant expresses their work in a way that is personal to them, so that what is written here represents the way I express this ministry; it is my individual response to this role.

What differentiates the funeral rite for the suicide and their family?

There are strong social and spiritual dynamics present at a funeral for one who has ended their life by *their own hand* that are not present at any other funeral rite.

It is over fifty years since suicide was decriminalized in the UK in 1961. The social consequences of that situation are still present today. As such, a suicide death still carries considerable social stigma, with people making derogatory comments about the deceased or remarks laying blame for the death at the door of those closest to the one bereaved. For those with a belief in an afterlife, even though this may not be linked to any particular religion, there can be many fears, not least that the person who has taken their life is lost forever with no hope of redemption. The funeral is a time when the bereaved have an increased sense of vulnerability because they cannot be sure of the comments and reactions of the mourners in relation to the social and spiritual realities mentioned. Alongside these anxieties, there are many uncertainties about how to express their bereavement. It is in the context of these dynamics specific to the funeral rite for one who has ended their own life that the Civil Celebrant must tread with respect and sensitivity towards the deceased and the bereaved.

Preparing and engaging in the funeral ceremony for the individual who has taken their own life and the family left behind

It is my belief that, for any funeral rite, personal preparation is as important as the time and preparation given to the family and the formulation of the funeral ceremony. My underlying spirituality is based on the Gospel of St. John and the message that runs throughout that Gospel, of Christ being the light of life, the bread of life, the water of life, and so on, and that God's life is most fully expressed in the love that we show one another, "I give you a new commandment; love one another; such as my love has been for you, so must your love be for each other."[4]

So, my first premise is to bring God's love into a situation of deep hurt and feelings of rejection felt by the family closest to the bereaved. This does not necessarily require the name of God to be spoken or preached. It requires the lived compassion that Jesus always showed to all who suffered. Only through personal prayer and a daily encounter with Jesus can God's compassion and love live in us. So for me, time of prayer, silence, and stillness are essential elements in my own life that underpin my ministry as a Civil Celebrant and are part of my preparation for the funeral rite.

4. John 13:34

The second premise is to be non-judgmental toward the deceased and their family. "Do not judge, and you will not be judged."[5] There are many interpretations about the causes and reasons for people ending their lives. However, the fact is that the only person who can give the answer is the deceased, and they are unable to tell us why they felt compelled towards an act of self-destruction. On speaking to some of those who have made a non-fatal suicide attempt, a recurring theme seems to be that the individual has a level of emotional pain so great that the natural instinct for survival is completely blotted out, and the only relief to their pain is death. However, since there are no definitive answers in a fatal attempt, leave judgement to God, and if you have any prejudice in your heart towards the deceased or the bereaved, then it is important to consider whether you are the right person to conduct the funeral. You are there to give dignity to all the good things in the life of the deceased, not to focus on or make judgements on the manner of their death.

The third premise is to listen attentively not only to the words spoken by the family, but to the emotions and unspoken dynamics that are at play between those involved in planning the funeral rite. I always ask the family to decide on a theme for the funeral service, which helps them to choose appropriate music, poetry, readings, words of consolation, or prayers. You may find you have to help family members listen to each other and to recognize each other's needs. Writer Hugh Elliott sums up the quality of listening needed, "Listen. Do not have an opinion while you listen because frankly, your opinion doesn't hold much water outside of Your Universe. Just listen. Listen until their brain has been twisted like a dripping towel and what they have to say is all over the floor."[6]

When everything they have said is metaphorically "all over the floor" but literally in your mind and on your notepad, you then have the material with which to put together the funeral rite and a tribute that will reflect the needs of the bereaved and honor the deceased.

What follows is the type of funeral rite that evolves from this process. All of the names and situations in this sample funeral rite are purely fictional, but the style is informed from my lived experience of being a Funeral Celebrant.

---

5. Luke 6:37
6. Hugh, "Quotable Quote."

Background Information

The deceased	Ruth
Age	48
Status	Divorcee
Children	Three children: Tim (age 22), Myra (age 20), Robin (age 16)
Former Husband	Keith (age 50)
Parents	Jim (age 72), Margaret (age 70)
Siblings	Brian (age 44), Jenny (age 40)

Ruth's Character

- Talented cellist, member of a regional orchestra
- Music teacher—well known locally for production of musicals in the school and for identifying talented musicians and helping young people reach a high standard of musical ability and develop latent talent
- Fun loving
- Devoted mum and a caring daughter towards her parents
- Became depressed after the break-up of the marriage two years ago but was having counselling and seemed to be coping

Circumstances of Death

Left school as usual on a Friday evening, but instead of going home, drove 160 miles to a seaside resort much loved by the family and visited frequently at the time the children were young. Walked into the sea. Body washed up three weeks later several miles down the coast (note: it is very important not to pry into the circumstances of the death but just allow the family to share what they can)

Key Family Dynamics

- Ruth was brought up in an active Baptist family. She did not continue her involvement once married, as her husband, Keith, had no affiliation to any religion, and he did not want the children brought up with a specific religious belief. Ruth and Keith agreed that they believed in the existence of God as a source of goodness and power at the center of creation and brought up their children with that belief. They also taught them that an essential characteristic of living was to respect and care for each other in the family and for those less fortunate than themselves.
- In adult life, Ruth was inspired by the Sufi tradition, and her daughter, Myra, has also followed this way of thinking.
- Parents are still practicing Baptists.
- Keith, Tim, and Robin have no particular religious persuasion and are not really sure whether they believe in an afterlife.

Theme of the Funeral

Three strands emerged on which all of the family agreed:

- To celebrate all the good things in Ruth's life
- To express the family's shock and bewilderment at the way Ruth died
- To include some religious aspect to the funeral in respect for Ruth's parents, for whom their Baptist life is very important

Because Ruth was well known and loved, the family decided that they would have a private funeral for the immediate family and friends and a separate memorial service for the wider social circle. From this background, the following ceremony evolved.

The Funeral Ceremony

Music on entry to the chapel

The cello piece "The Swan" from the *Carnival of the Animals* by C. Saint-Saëns was chosen because it was piece of music Ruth loved from childhood. The family felt that the melancholy tone of the music was appropriate to the sadness they felt at Ruth's death.[7]

The over-riding memory of Ruth before the tragedy of her death is a person wonderfully talented, warm, and loving, who would always make time for others. Her favorite mantra was, *we only get one shot at life, so live it the best you can and always have time to care for people.* Ruth certainly lived by this code, and it is with sadness that today those of you closest to her are having to say goodbye with so many unanswered questions and with the deep pain of loss in your hearts.

Poems, Readings, and Prayers

In order to express some of that sadness, I am first of all going to light the large candle you see here on my right. The candle represents the huge loss felt by Ruth's death, and the flame represents the love and warmth she gave during her life.

I will now read a poem which Ruth's children received from a family friend and which they have chosen because it represents something of the experience of their mother's death.

Ruth was brought up in the Baptist tradition, and while she was not actively involved in church life after her teenage years, she always felt that those years of being in the Baptist church influenced her throughout her life. Jim and Margaret have selected a short phrase from the bible to be read which expresses their trust in God's love and mercy towards their daughter. Before the reading, we will light the second candle, which represents Jim and Margaret's love and loss for their daughter. The reading is from the Prophet Daniel, "But yours, O Lord, our God, are compassion and forgiveness! Yet we rebelled against you . . . "[8]

The third candle represents Ruth's interest in Sufism, and her daughter Myra, who also finds inspiration in the Sufism tradition, is

---

7. *The first part of this eulogy reviews Ruth's childhood through her marriage. The selection below includes the essence of the eulogy—Ed.*

8. Dan 9:9

going to read from Rumi's great works of poetry, Masnavi Book IV, "This world is like a dream, but you, the sleeper, imagine it is real."[9]

Finally, I will light the fourth candle. This represents a time for the silent thoughts or prayers of all of you present here. It is time for you to remember Ruth in the specific way she was important to you. This will be followed by Beethoven's *Variations on Piano Concerto No. 5 Adagio.*

Words of Commendation

The immediate family now gathers round Ruth and place a hand on her coffin for the words of commendation which they repeat after the funeral celebrant.

Ruth, we give thanks that we walked life's path with you.

We are sorry that we could not prevent your tragic death.

In the bow and string of the cello, we will remember you.

In the pain of our loss, we will remember you.

In fond memories, we will remember you.

In the heart of life, we will remember you.

As long as we live, we will miss your presence.

But in our hearts, your place is assured for always.

Committal

Please stand.

To complete this last rite of Ruth's earthly life,

We now commend her body to its natural end.

May her spirit live on in the hearts of you who love her.

Leave this place in peace, knowing you have acknowledged your love and respect for Ruth.

Dwell not on the manner of her death

But find comfort in the manner of her living.

And for those who live in faith, be comforted by the belief that Ruth will be received into the endless loving mercy of God.

Final music: "Song of the Seashore"

This flute piece is a Japanese lullaby. It was chosen because the flute was another musical instrument loved by Ruth. She left this life by the seashore, and the words of this lullaby are of someone walking by the seashore remembering someone dearly loved whom they have lost in death.

9. Rumi, "Quotable Quote."

Bibliography

Ashworth, Jacinta, and Ian Farthing. *Churchgoing in the UK: A Research Report from Tearfund on Church Attendance in the UK.* Teddington: Tearfund, 2007.

Barley, Linda. *Christian Roots, Contemporary Spirituality.* London: Church House Publishing, 2006.

Elliot, Hugh. "Quotable Quote." Goodreads. http://www.goodreads.com/quotes/36341-do-not-have-an-opinion-while-you-listen-because-frankly

Rumi. "Quotable Quote." Goodreads. http://www.goodreads.com/quotes/438012-this-place-is-a-dream-only-a-sleeper-considers-it.

Young, Michael. "The Dead Citizens Charter." Powerbase. March 29, 2010. http://powerbase.info/index.php/The_Dead_Citizens_Charter.

Eulogy for Evan
May 23, 2013, 14 Sivan 5773

Rabbi Adam J. Raskin, Congregation Har Shalom

I went into Evan's bedroom a few days ago. After hearing so many stories about Evan, after seeing so many pictures and listening to so many vignettes about his life from friends and family members, I felt that I just needed to quietly be in a place where I might be able to sense Evan's presence; I wanted to inhabit a space where he lived, where he dreamed, where he found some peace and quiet. Evan's room is a sanctuary to everything he loved in life. Now, I don't want to give any false impressions. This sanctuary had its share of clothing piles and half consumed bottles of Gatorade, and no, the bed was not made. On the walls, however, there is a shrine to his beloved Washington Capitals—banners, jerseys, posters—in another corner, RGIII, in another, Yankee stadium. Around the perimeter are countless golden trophies all in the same pose—in fact, it is the very same pose as the picture so many of you have made into your Facebook profile pictures or put up on your Facebook walls in tribute to Evan, the elongated body of a basketball player in the midst of taking his shot, arms extended above his head, feet barely touching the ground, face and eyes fixed on the basket. On the table near his bed was a partially eaten bag of *mandelbread*, a delicious treat his grandma made for him. Out of the corner of my eye, I spotted Evan's navy blue bar mitzvah yarmulke stamped with the date November 14, 2009 sitting there on his night table next to his bed. I wondered, *did he put it on his head to say Shema before he went to bed?* On top of some random papers sat his gleaming new 2013 Churchill High School yearbook.

I picked it up, flipping through its shiny pages, thinking about Thursday evening's remarkable vigil in the Churchill gym. Every seat was filled, every bleacher extended to its full capacity, a sea of kids all wearing white shirts, one after the other coming forward to the microphone to speak about how much Evan meant to them. Fighting back tears that sometimes overcame them, each one related their own memories of Evan, a story, an encounter, a funny episode. Some had been friends since kindergarten; others came into Evan's life more recently, but each remarked about how Evan's most recognizable feature was not his 6'3" stature but his characteristic smile. Friend

29

after friend, classmate after classmate, teammate after teammate invariably mentioned that smile that will be emblazoned on all of our hearts and in all of our memories. He was born with that smile, you know. Susan's brother Howard used to stand over Evan's crib and say over and over, *stop smiling, Evan; stop smiling, Evan,* and little baby Evan would giggle and laugh and smile even more. Is it possible for one person to have 1,000 best friends? It seemed that Evan's smile made everyone consider him their best friend. Whether it was the smile he flashed to you while passing in the hallway or his smile after he checked you on the basketball court or his smile while celebrating a win by the Caps or while watching a movie and eating candy with Allison, his smile was his most identifiable feature, his most endearing feature, and, I believe, the picture of Evan that most of us will have in our minds as we remember him and think about him for a very long time to come.

Just before I turned to leave Evan's room, I noticed a yellow post-it-note on the mirror above his dresser. On it was a handwritten note from his mom. She wrote it just after Evan's back surgery, and he was trying to catch up on some of the school work he missed while he was recovering. In the kindest, most loving and reassuring words, Susan wrote to him not to worry about anything. If his grades slipped a little during this time, it would be totally understandable. Just try your hardest, she told him. That's all she expected. With reassurances of her unconditional support, she signed it, *Love Mom.* As he got up every morning and applied the array of deodorants, aftershaves, and skin cleansers lined up below that mirror, I imagine that Evan began each day by reading that note stuck to the mirror. He started each day knowing how much his parents loved him, how he had these two remarkable, adoring sisters, Allison and Shelby, and his beloved grandparents, and so many friends.

And that is just one reason why being here today is so maddening, so perplexing! Here is a kid who was adored by so many, who had a loving family and countless friends. How is it possible that we are burying him today? You know, we are remarkable, complex creatures, you and I. The human body is a marvel and an absolutely amazing, ingenious creation. Evan's own towering physique is a testimony to that. Look at all that we can do. Look at all we can build and accomplish. We are beautifully and wonderfully made. But as much as we know about our bodies, as cutting-edge and sophisticated as science and biomedical advances are in this day and age, the mind remains a mysterious frontier. Oh, there are theories and schools of thought. There are hypotheses and speculations, but how and why the mind works is still such an incredible enigma. How did it happen that Evan's mind turned a blind eye to all this love and support on that fateful Monday morning? What was this inscrutable cloak that descended over his awareness that no matter what pain he was suffering, no matter what was terrorizing him, that there would always be another way, another answer, another source of relief and comfort—anything but this. Anything but the answer he was deceived into believing was the only way out. We will never have all the answers, dear friends. And I know that so many of you have already tried to put the pieces of this puzzle together. You have wracked your brains, analyzed your conversations, attempted to decipher hidden meanings in texts or messages, and that's normal. We are all searching for some glimmer of meaning in this chaos. But at some point, we have to stop asking ourselves if we might have overlooked a hint or failed to pick up on some indicator that this would happen. Last night, we had social workers here to facilitate a grief support group for teens and their parents. One of the social workers said that it is indeed common to ask ourselves these questions, to wonder if we could have known something or done something to stop this, to put ourselves on trial. But, she said, it has to be a fair trial. It has to be a fair trial. As you attempt to remember and reconstruct the weeks and days leading up to this, please be fair to yourselves. There is not one person here who wouldn't have rushed to Evan's side to prevent this if we knew what was going on in the deep recesses of his mind. You know that, and I know that. It is natural to ask ourselves these questions, but please, please be fair to yourself when you do.

As we contemplate the very difficult, very painful days and weeks that lie ahead, I want you to think about words that we will encounter in this week's Torah portion. Suffering his own disillusionment, frustration, and pain, Moses approaches God in total exasperation. And God says to the worn down leader, *lo tisa atah l'vadecha.* You do not have to bear this burden alone. God instructs Moses to appoint seventy elders from the tribes of Israel to help him bear the heavy load of leadership. *Lo tisa atah l'vadecha.* You do not have to bear this alone.[10] And I say those same words to all of you. You are not alone. You are never alone. Every one of us is surrounded by a loving community of friends, teachers, spiritual leaders, parents, family members, countless people who care about you and love you, and together, we will help each other. We will bear each other's burdens of sorrow,

---

10. Num 11:17

and we will walk together through this dark valley of the shadow of death. And as we do, let us hold each other closer than ever. Let us learn to pay close attention to each other, and let us learn how to find the people in our lives we can talk to when we are stricken with grief or confusion. Evan, you know, was always looking out for everyone else. He was always concerned about what other people needed or how he could include someone else in his warm embrace. He wasn't a self-promoter. In fact, his mom speculated to me that Evan would have probably grown up to be a teacher or a coach, constantly giving of himself to support other people. So let us take up that legacy as our own in Evan's memory, in honor of Evan's legacy. Let us be as vigilant about other people's needs as we are our own. Let us look out for others at least as much as we look out for ourselves. And let us always remember the radiant smile of Evan, and may his memory illuminate our hearts, and be an inspiration for goodness in each one of us for many years to come.

Yehi zichro baruch—May Evan's memory always be a blessing. Amen

∽

Homily for a Suicide From Depression

Reverend John D. Corbett, OP, PhD

"So stop passing judgement before the time of his return. He will bring light to what is hidden in darkness and manifest the intentions of hearts. At that time, everyone will receive his praise from God."[11]

Today, we mourn the loss of our sister Sarah, who left us last Thursday night. She had been battling depression for over twenty years and, seeing no end to her struggle, opted for what I am sure she hoped would be a final solution to her pain.

There is no need to hide the fact that this is for us a most bitter moment. We were with her in her struggles. We listened for long hours. We scanned the horizon with her for a sign, any sign, that her long vigil in darkness would end and that the morning would bring light for her eyes, color to her world, and warmth midst life's winter. We wanted her depression's siege to vanish into the dawn like a defeated enemy. But we could not convince her that this was to be. Instead, it is she who has vanished from our sight.

Before we can see this moment in light, we must acknowledge the darkness we are in now. We must face our worst fear. What has happened to Sarah? I don't mean what happened to her over the course of her lifetime to bring her to the conviction that suicide was her best option. I mean what happened to her soul in her moment of judgment as she left this world? Suicide is considered by some a great sin, and it is considered especially dangerous because there is but little opportunity for repentance once the transgression is underway. We must face our worst fear head on. Did Sarah die out of favor with God?

Speaking as her pastor, I simply cannot believe that she did. For a sin to be committed, there must be ill will, and I can testify from many conversations with her and with her loved ones that there was no such ill will within her. There are people who are deeply wounded with anger and who see death by suicide as a way of punishing those left behind.

Sarah was not like that. On the contrary, she loved her family and friends and wished for them to be spared in her long night of pain. She

---

11. 1 Cor 4:4–5

knew they sorrowed in her sorrow, and I believe that, in her mind, putting an end to her own suffering here on earth would also serve to free her family and friends from further pain. She was wrong about this. Her friends would gladly have continued to watch the nights with her, and her decision to end her own life only deepened the darkness and increased the burden that her family carries. Yet, a decision can be fatally mistaken and still be in good faith, can still come from a good heart. And God looks, above all, at the heart.

There are those few who are convinced that they own their lives the way they own their cars and their cats and that they are free in principle to do anything they please to their own bodies. They believe that their dominion over themselves is absolute and unqualified and that God's sovereignty stops at the point where their minds and bodies begin. Such people have a mortal fear of God as the enemy of their freedom and so refuse him a place in their lives lest he not be content with a part and should, like a tyrant, seize the whole. For such people, suicide is ultimate self-assertion, and it is, indeed, difficult to reconcile suicide as self-assertion with death as self-surrender to God's saving will.

But Sarah was not like this. She was not claiming to be the Lord of Life. She was seeking the Lord of Life, seeking God's mercy, seeking God's peace, seeking God's face. She believed that in leaving this world of pain, she would find herself again-safe in the arms of the Good Shepherd. She would never have left this world behind if she had not believed that, in doing so, she would meet her Savior.

Was she right about this? We must tread *carefully* here. We can never know for sure what is in someone else's mind and heart. I have spoken of Sarah's own state of mind, and what I have said does seem to me to be true. But all I can offer on that account is a human word. I can never know for sure someone else's state of soul, or, to say the same thing, I can never be quite certain of the state of someone else's relationship with God. For that matter, I cannot even be absolutely certain of my own. St. Paul writes to the Corinthians that he does not presume to judge even himself, and he firmly admonishes his congregation not "to pass judgment before the time."[12] Happily, we cannot presume to condemn but, less happily, neither can we presume to acquit. Judgment is the Lord's and the Lord's alone. For this reason, I have always been hesitant to join in the humanly-quite-understandable

12. Ibid.

34

tendency in funeral liturgies to canonize the recently deceased. Judgment is the Lord's.

So, even though Sarah appeared to me a victim and decidedly not a perpetrator, even though her love and goodness were transparent to me, even though her disease seemed to have pushed her *choice* to end her life well beyond the boundaries of moral responsibility, still the ground of our own hope for her salvation does not lie in her innocence. Rather, it lies in the limitless power and limitless mercy of God manifested in the death and resurrection of Christ.

Thomas Merton once wrote, "When anyone is judged by God, he receives in the hour of judgment a gift from God. The gift that is offered him, in his judgment, is *truth*. He can receive the truth or reject it; but in any case truth is being offered silently, mercifully."[13] The implication of this remark is that God's judgment is *not* like the work of an accountant whose mind works in a climate of neutrality and whose will and personal preferences are left to the side as the final figure is tallied. Rather the communication of the final truth of this human life is always offered through the medium of divine mercy so that the *acceptance* of the judgment of God is at the same time the acceptance of the divine context of mercy and forgiveness in which it is always clothed.

Theologians have been accustomed to think of the final judgment, the final coming of Christ, as more or less the summing up and making public of all the individual verdicts passed on all of the individuals who have been born since the world began. But what if this were reversed? What if we look on God's dealing with each of us individually in the light of what God intends to do for us all on the last day? Since Jesus is outside of time as we understand it, our final encounter with God's mercy in the moment of our death and our judgment would be an anticipation of the form and character of God's *great deed* that the Lord will do for us on the last day, *not a deed of destruction and revenge but of mercy and life.*

So we hope and believe it is for Sarah. She knew this world's darkness at greater depth than most of us ever will. We sense that she never despaired of God's presence or of his mercy. Although she had the resources to face on her own the prospects of a life of unremitting grey, she was unable to find them in time. However, she was and is God's child and will be open to God's light which will shatter her darkness in the dawn of Christ's resurrection.

13. Merton, *Conjectures of a Guilty Bystander*, 68

What is our role now for our sister? How can we help her? We believe in the power of prayer. When we ask for help in the name of the Lord Jesus and in the power of the Holy Spirit, God the Father listens and then acts. More than this, we believe that *our own prayer and love* can by the power of the Holy Spirit sent by the Father and the Son, penetrate and share in the healing of the heart of the dead. Why? Because we believe in the communion of saints, past and present. We are not first of all individuals who are then gathered into a sort of assembly that we call Church. Rather, we are first of all the Church, the Body of Christ, which is today gathered together in special power in this Eucharist in behalf of Sarah. In this unity we stand and we stand in hopeful defiance of death's final claim. We stand convinced and convicted that our prayers and love can speed our sister on her way to heaven. We do not claim to understand all that is involved in this mystery that Catholics call purgatory. But we believe that God's judgment on her reflects God's original intent for her and this saving intent will transform even those things which stood in her way into portals of grace, shattering the darkness, bringing her God's transformative love, bringing her to heaven. Eternal light shine upon her, O Lord. May her soul and the souls of all the faithful departed, through the mercy of God, rest in peace. Amen.

Bibliography

Merton, Thomas. *Conjectures of a Guilty Bystander*. Garden City, NY: Doubleday, 1966.

Michael G.'s Eulogy
November 24, 2007

Reverend Dennis W. Spence

Michael died while dealing with a medical issue. The first part of this eulogy contains the history of Michel G.'s birth, childhood, and marriage. We have condensed the original and included the essence of the eulogy.—Ed.

After the wedding, Michael returned to seminary at Midwestern in Kansas City to complete his studies. He began doing ministry in the United Methodist Church and found it to his liking. He was ordained as an elder in the United Methodist church in 1992. He served faithfully in Huntsville, Magazine, Ola/Plainview, Hughes/Widener, Clarendon/Holly Grove, Parker's Chapel in El Dorado, Pleasant Grove, and finally, the Rowell Circuit, consisting of Union, Prosperity, and Mt. Olivet.

A few weeks ago, when Michael was so ill, he reminisced about a few of his favorite things, of course, his family—his wife, LuAnn, daughter, Arrie, and his grandchildren. It was in his blood to be a devoted family man.

Nature and travel also energized Michael. Armed with a camera, he could lose himself in the wonder of God's creation. His trip to Greece a few years ago was the "trip of a lifetime," to use his own words. To journey where Christianity began to take root and flourish and marvel at the breathtaking views of ancient Greece was a rare treat. He also pointed out that the annual family reunion at Mount Eagle Retreat Center was a taste of heaven on earth. To be with family, to travel to a scenic location, and to be immersed in the natural beauty of God's world in a relaxed atmosphere was a taste of heaven.

Without question, Michael was called to be a minister of God who proclaimed the good news of Jesus Christ. He loved the church. It was in his DNA. It was the sparkle in his eye. It was his life. He would not want to do anything to hurt his relationship with his family, his church family, or his eternal relationship with God in Christ.

In light of his deep-seated beliefs and values, his death at such a young age and the circumstances of his dying has been difficult to understand. Many of you are aware of his own involvement in his death. The family has graciously allowed me to address this today in the hopes that it might minister to those of us who are hurting.

Michael had a good heart. He had a big and generous heart. Yet, he had a defective physical heart. He was seriously ill the last few months with a disease that could not be diagnosed. He had episodes when he would not be responsive. Some say we really lost him on September 29 because he was not fully himself after that. He was doing better after the pacemaker was put in, but he was not well. He was not in his right mind—or his right heart—when he made the decision that he did.

The United Methodist Church does not condone the taking of one's life. I personally believe this approach might not be right, for this condemnation leaves a heavy burden on those left behind. In our church's mission, we seek to do all we can to help people see the hope that is there in the midst of despair and pain. We only wish that Michael had only been open to the other choices that were available to him, i.e., hospice and their compassion and how they keep people pain free. Yet, we have compassion for Michael, who has taken this journey. We do not judge him. We have not walked in his shoes, nor have we leaned on his crutches. Our church does not believe that one questionable choice in a weak moment negates all the wise decisions made day in and day out for fifty years.

Let me remind you that our relationship with God is more about God's grace than our goodness. Michael was as good a man as I know. Yet, even all his goodness is not enough to have an eternal relationship with God. Michael was not in a loving relationship with God because Michael was so good. He was and is in a relationship with God because God is good and gracious and giving and forgiving. Michael was as good as he was because he accepted an invitation to dance with God in Christ. His goodness was a way of saying thanks for his free gift of salvation, not a way of earning salvation. *We are saved by faith, not works.*[14]

Michael felt he was living a plan that came from God. He walked with God. He lived for God. He died in Christ. I believe that he is getting the answers now that he did not have then. He is having his conversation with God. He is in the loving arms of Almighty God. Thanks be to God. May we seek God's guidance in how we are to live out the rest of our lives!

---

14. Eph 2:8–9

A Funeral Homily
A Young Suicide

Father William Bausch

As I look out over this congregation brought here by the common bond of the tragic death of someone we knew, I know that words are inadequate to temper our grief. Therefore, I shall try to make my words brief and address them to three groups of people. The first words concern John; the second concern John's friends and peers and classmates who are here—to the great credit of your friendship and sympathy for his family—in great numbers; and the third concern all of us, but especially John's family.

As for John, I presume that no one here is unaware that he took his own life. I think we ought to say that out loud so that we can hear it publicly and not just whisper this open secret among ourselves and so that we can try to deal with it. But I want to share with you that, often, this deed, in the confused mind of a troubled person, is done out of love, a misguided and wrong-headed love, but love nevertheless.

The thinking of a person who is deeply troubled frequently goes like this: I am hurting so deeply, and am so depressed, and I have tried everything, and the only way I can stop the hurt is to end my life. Also, I am a burden. I'm hurting the people I love. I'm in the way. I'm making a mess of things. I'm unhappy and making others unhappy. I worry those nearest to me. It would be kinder for everyone if I took the burden off their shoulders, if I weren't here, if I ceased to be. That's the understandable but backwards logic that often is at work in a person so troubled he or she doesn't see or think clearly.

And that's at least good to know. It's at least good to know that, as painful as suicide is for us, at the bottom, there is the truth that it is often done out of love and concern for others. It's not good thinking, but bad thinking that nevertheless has its roots in charity, not malice. And we ought to remember that about John. His tender love, as he understood it, did him in.

As for you young people here in such great numbers, John's friends and companions, for you, John's death raises a question. It is this, what are you going to do about your friend's death? I mean, after the pain and the shock, after the anger—maybe at John himself, probably at God—after the hurt and tears, what are you going to do about your friend's death? It's easy to cry in his memory. What are you going to do with your life in his memory when your tears have dried?

. . . What are you going to do about John's death? To whom will you turn when your pain is overwhelming you from this loss? Can you do what John did not and reach out to your family, a counsellor, a teacher and share the terrible hurt? Then, as the pain subsides, as it does with mourning, I would encourage you to ask the question, what am I going to do about his unfinished masterpiece? Will it be, in a month or so, life as usual? Or can you build on his humor, his ability, his fun, and his unrealized dreams? I would suggest that if there is any fitting response to the shock of your friend's death, it is life, your life, a life that's lived better, a life lived more selflessly, a life that makes a difference, a life that is honest and decent, a life that makes beautiful music for John and for the Lord. Across the chasm of death, you can make John live. The music doesn't have to stop here today and doesn't have to be buried with John. You have your choice.

Finally, to all of you, to all of us, but especially to John's family, in this sad moment I leave you with an image of hope, of perspective. Picture yourselves standing on a dock beside one of those great old-time sailing vessels. It's standing there, sails folded, waiting for the wind. Suddenly, a breeze comes up. When the captain senses the breeze as a forerunner of the necessary wind, he quickly orders the sails to be let down and, sure enough, the wind comes, catches the sails full force, and carries the ship away from the dock where you are standing.

Inevitably, you or someone on that dock is bound to say, *well, there she goes!* And from our point of view, it indeed does go. Soon the mighty ship, laden with its crew and goods, is on the horizon where water and sky meet, and it looks like a speck before it disappears. It's still mighty and grand, still filled with life and goods, but it's left us. We're standing on the dock quite alone. But on the other side of the ocean, people are standing in anticipation, and as that speck on the horizon becomes larger and larger, they begin to cry something different. They are crying with joy, not abandonment, *here she comes!* And at the landing, there is welcome, joy, embracing, and celebration.

We miss John. He is quickly receding from our sight, and this funeral and his burial at the cemetery are our farewells, our versions of *there he goes.* But goes where? From our sight, from our embrace, from our care and love and friendship? How we miss that, how we will miss him! We hurt, for he should not have left us so early! He could have waited and should have waited for a stronger breeze, for better tides. We must remember on faith that *here he comes* is the cry on the eternal shore, where Jesus, who understands the human heart even when it goes wrong, is waiting. And there is John, now forever larger than life, filled with life, intoxicated with life and laughter, and in the arms of the One who makes all things new again, the One who says, *welcome, John. Welcome home.* But, perhaps he also says, *I could have waited! But here you are—welcome*"

Death Provides

Reverend Ron Edmondson

On behalf of the family of Hunter, I wish to thank each one of you for being here today. Your presence indicates something. It indicates your love for this family—and for Hunter. It's been a long week. You're tired. Some are confused—certainly disappointed. And though today is a very difficult day, the Bible makes some promises.

> God is our refuge and our strength, an ever-present help in distress. Therefore we fear not, though the earth be shaken and mountains plunge into the depths of the sea; Though its waters rage and foam and the mountains quake at its surging.[15]

And the Bible also says,

> Who will separate us from the love of Christ? Trial, or distress, or persecution, or hunger, or nakedness, or danger, or the sword? . . . Yet in all this we are more than conquerors because of him who has loved us.[16]

For I am convinced that neither death, nor life, nor angels, nor principalities, nor things present, nor things to come, nor powers, nor height, nor depth, nor any other created thing will be able to separate us from the love of God, which is in Christ Jesus our Lord.

Hunter Lane M., born March 2, 2000, passed away on December 2, 2014. He was a dearly loved son, brother, grandson, nephew, and friend

Psalm 127 says, "Children are a gift from the Lord; the fruit of the womb is a reward."[17] Hunter is cherished by his all who know him . . .

So, A child is born.

A child is raised.

Friends are made.

And no one could have predicted this day.

Life happens in a moment, good or bad.

And today, we remember and celebrate the good times with Hunter.

---

15. Ps 46:1–3

16. Rom 8:35, 37

17. Ps 127:3

Words of Family Members

Note: In this section, family members are called upon to reflect on Hunter.
We all probably have the same question, *why*?

The wisest man of all times wrote in Ecclesiastes 3, "There is an appointed time for everything, and a time for every affair under the heavens. A time to be born, and a time to die."[18]

There is a time for everything.

Death, especially, provides a time for questions and confusion.

Why?

Why so soon?

Why now?

Why Hunter?

Death also provides a time of sorrow.

We'll miss his physical presence.

We'll miss his smile.

We'll miss the laughs he created.

Death is also, though—as hard as it is to accept—to be a time for hope.
For those who follow the person of Christ, death is not an ending; it's a change of location.

Death is a sobering event. You don't know how to feel or how to respond. You're hurting. Someone you love is gone, and you don't know what to do about it.

But, finally, *death provides us with a time for reflection.*

We are reminded that life is fragile, that we should protect it, that every moment matters, that we should live it well. We should live like tomorrow is uncertain—because it is. And, in a sobering kind of way, we are reminded at death that God is real. and that we should get to know him. Hebrews 4:7 says, "Today, if you should hear his voice, harden not your hearts."

I'm often asked at a time like this, *how can you be sure someone is in Heaven?* And—I have to be honest—ultimately, I can only answer for me; you can only answer for you.

Hunter's grandmother shared deeply personal conversations she had with Hunter—Spiritual conversations. She asked him all the right questions. Based on his responses, Hunter had a faith that Jesus Christ is Lord,

---

18. Eccl 3:1–2

and that's why the Scripture says, "O death, where is your sting?"[19] Because, though in presence Hunter is not here, he is fully present with the Lord.

So, I'm confident Hunter would say to us today,

- I love you.

- I'm okay. In fact, I'm better than ever.

- Heaven is a great place. He might even say they have something far better than X-Box.

Today, Hunter is celebrating the laughter and the joy and the glory of Heaven with all those loved ones of faith who have gone on before us.

Randy Alcorn in his book, *Heaven,* says, "Your relationship with your loved one hasn't ended. It's just been interrupted."[20]

Place your hope and trust in Jesus Christ, and you'll see Hunter again.

Bibliography

Alcorn, Randy C. *Heaven.* Carol Stream, IL: Tyndale House Publishers, 2007.

---

19. 1 Cor 15:55
20. Alcorn, *Heaven*

Serving Jewish Families of Suicide

Helping Them Make Their Memories a Blessing in the Midst of Tragedy, Anger, Shame and Guilt, Part I: Thoughts from Two Rabbi Survivors of Family Suicide

Rabbis Chaya Gusfield and Lori Klein

Accompanying and Giving Voice to the Family

The *hesped* (eulogy) can be a powerful inspiration for surviving friends and family to begin to make meaning of their loved one's suicide. To illustrate this point, we have included a sample *hesped*, one that could have been written after the suicide of a young woman. A brief analysis of the *hesped* follows.

Eulogy/Hesped for Julia Zoe G., Born February. 8, 1949, Died Memorial Day, 1970

We gather to mourn the tragic death of Julia Zoe G. We were not supposed to be here today. This is not ok! We feel so many turbulent emotions. Let those emotions rise and honor each of them as your heart's response to this moment.

We may even feel judgment and anger at Julie. This is normal. This is expected. But who are we to judge the pain of another? Thank G-d there is only one true judge. *Baruch Dayan HaEmet.* Blessed is the one who is the *true* judge, the One who judges with compassion.

We may never understand completely why Julie ended her life on the threshold of adulthood. Today, we do not even try to understand the unanswerable *whys*. This is the heart of today's challenge, to understand there is no knowing what is unknowable. Not today. Not tomorrow. The sages wrote, *Let us not seek to understand what is too difficult for us, nor search for what is hidden, nor be preoccupied with what is beyond, for we have been shown more than we can comprehend.*[21] We grieve, instead, from the center of sorrowful mystery.

The Hebrew word for funeral, *levaya*, means accompaniment. Today, let us accompany Julie as we try to understand her pain. Let us accompany

---

21. Ps 131:1

Julie's family in their anguish and grief, her parents Robert and Ruth, her brother David, her sister Irene. Let us accompany each other as we begin our painful steps forward from this moment.

Julie was bright, creative, and playful. She played the flute. She loved beads. She loved the ballet. The first child of Robert and Ruth, they loved her well and took care of her. Julie and her family traveled to India when she was twelve, and they had many adventures there. She carried with her the dazzling array of colors, smells, and landscapes, as well as the harshness of the poverty she saw there. She complained the servants got in the way with their helpfulness and eagerness to please!

We will never know everything Julie might have accomplished and experienced had she lived past the age of twenty-one. Julie was eager for life and more life, yet she also was ill. As a society, we do not yet know how to effectively treat the kind of mental illness Julie endured until she could endure it no more. We grieve for what could have been, what we hoped would have been, for the future that no longer offers us hope for health. We grieve for uncelebrated birthdays and *simchas* that will never be. We grieve for dreams that were never fulfilled, for joy that never returned.

In this week's Torah portion, *Shelach L'cha*,[22] "Send Forth," the Israelites who had been delivered from Egypt by G-d learn G-d will not permit them to enter the Promised Land. Instead, they will die in the wilderness, some of them soon, some of them after years of wandering. We learn from their story that, sometimes, we have no control over the length of our journey or where it will take us. Sometimes, we cannot choose to leave the wilderness or enter the Promised Land. Julie wanted to leave the confines and wilderness of her illness, but she could not. My heart aches with compassion for her struggles and the struggle of her family, who did *everything* they knew how to help her find her way home. *Everything.*

These are turbulent and confusing times, with great social change and conflicts surrounding the Vietnam War. We are experimenting with new ways of being in the world and even in our minds. We don't really know how much these social changes affected Julie. She so wanted a normal life, but during these times, she didn't know what a normal life should look like.

An 18th century rabbi in Germany, Ezekiel Katzenellenbogen, once said that every life contains some *Torah*. Every life contains some teaching, some wisdom, some learning for us. In her way, Julie sought to bring more light into the world. After Julie left Beloit College and moved to Berkeley,

22. Num 13:1—15:41

she sold candles. The Proverbs[23] tell us, the human spirit is the light of G-d, *ner Adonai nishmat Adam*. Each of us contains Divine sparks. Julie's sparks have been released, and yet, they will still light our way through darkness of our memories, for Julie had so much light to give. May each of us carry her sparks with us.

Zichrona livracha, may Julie's memory be a blessing—a blessing. May Julie's family have the love and strength to continue to remember how her life touched and changed theirs. Forever.

Analysis of Hesped

This *hesped* accomplishes several functions. It finds the *Torah* residing within Julie and makes it visible for the mourners; thus, it helps the mourners begin to reclaim their more positive memories. The *hesped* gives the mourners permission to feel their emotions. The Talmud states a *hesped* functions not only to praise the deceased but also to encourage weeping and lamentation among the mourners.[24] After a death by suicide, family members will feel a large range of sometimes disturbing emotions. This *hesped* normalizes any emotion the mourners might feel. The *hesped* frames Julie's illness and suicide with compassion, modeling a non-judgmental and non-shaming attitude. Finally, the *hesped* gives friends and family something to "do" in the wake of this tragedy. They can accompany each other and assist each other toward finding meaning in their tragedy and healing. They can find ways to memorialize her through various constructive activities. They can find ways to try and prevent others from choosing such a way to die.

23. Prov 20:27

24. Babylonian Talmud, *Berachot* 6b

Funeral Sermon and Service for Depression

Reverend Kate Braestrup

Welcome and Invocation

Welcome, my friends, to a place made holy by your presence, a place made sacred by the very sorrow that weights your hearts. Wherever two or three are gathered in my name, Christ told us, God is with us.

Mourning is the bitter edge of love. Inevitably, it finds us, batters the hearts we wear upon our sleeves. To love another is, eventually, to taste tears.

But must this have come so soon, we ask? So soon! We cry, in sorrow and in anger also, shaking our fists at the sky. Why this? Why now? And it is bitter. And it hurts.

And still you come, today, and still you enter in, by the tread of your human feet creating sacred ground on which to walk. By your very tears and breath, you bless the air and make of this place sanctuary.

And so, let us welcome each other into the presence of that spirit who was known to our ancestors and shall be known to our descendants also by the name of God.

Here we are, in the presence of God.

Psalm 23

We can do no more than this today, and it is enough. Welcome, my friends, and thank you for being here.

Serenity Prayer

Music

"Round Our Skiff" by Carol Rohl
"Isle Au Haut Lullaby" by Gordon Bok

Homily

Sorrow has come to us.
   Let us accept it simply.
   Let us declare it plainly, in its effects and in its cause.

48

We weep, for unshed tears are stones upon the heart. We weep because Emily died. We weep because Emily died by her own hand.

If understanding is difficult to come by today, if you are disbelieving, remorseful, filled with pain or anger, or all of the above, you are in good company.

Despite the discourses of rational science and despite the analgesic of faith, any death retains its mystery and its sting. Suicide is particularly mysterious, and it stings cruelly.

Any death opens a gap in the fabric of our interwoven lives; this death rips a huge and ragged hole, one even the most skilled among us do not begin to know how to mend.

Even saying the words out loud is terrible and strange. Emily is no more. How can this be?

Couldn't she have stayed a little longer, stayed for one more view of Ragged Mountain glowing in the sun, one more skinny dip in the Baltic, one more glimpse of the star at the right from the deck of a wooden home that rocks on the ancient sea?

Wasn't she curious to know what new and perilous adventure her father might suggest, or what sort of colorful creation her mama might invent? Didn't she wonder, indeed, what could next emerge from her own encounters with paint and canvas, corks and duct tape? This, after all, was a young woman capable of making art and poetry out of grocery store price stickers and squashed mosquitoes. Surely her own work, the magic of her own mind, would be sufficiently entertaining for her to want to stay for more?

Oh, Emily. In life, you delighted us. What delight, what comfort, what one word or act or bribe might life have offered that would have held you here? We would have gladly given it, given all, if only we could have saved you.

Someone asked me this week how I would explain Emily's death to a young child. *I would tell the truth,* I answered. *I would say that Emily Ann S. died after a long illness.*

A friend describes the illness of clinical depression as a dark dragon that muscles onto a human soul. It is very difficult to shake him loose. Some of us in this very room may have come close enough to that dragon to feel his breath or to have been nicked by his claws. For one reason or another—and maybe it was sheer luck—we have so far managed to avoid that dragon's full and fiery embrace.

49

The dragon got a really good grip on Emily.

She fought back. She fought hard and long. In fact, I do believe that what was truest in Emily was still fighting all the way to the end. Sometimes, in the midst of her struggles, she reached for the wrong weapons. If you fight that dragon with alcohol, it only makes him stronger. Sometimes, she seemed to have mistaken her allies for enemies, fighting her parents, her doctor, or her boyfriend!

But Emily kept trying. She had a life worth fighting for, and she knew it. Do you doubt this? Look at her paintings. To paint beauty, you must be able to see beauty. Emily's paintings are beautiful. Look at her friends. To have such friends as these, you must be a good and loyal friend yourself. Emily had love. God knows she had love.

Incidentally, Emily must have received not only her talent but also her fiercely loving heart as an inheritance from her parents. If you have spent time with the family this week, you will have witnessed Kerry and John's extraordinary honesty, generosity, and strength. You will have seen how gentle they are with each other, how willing they are to give one another room to grieve, each in his own way. John, Kerry, Andre, and Maggie, you are magnificent. We love you.

It is tempting, when faced with so monstrous a loss, to try to pretty it up, to make it somehow romantic. *She was too good for this world*, we might say. There is ample encouragement in our culture for this sort of thing, *Romeo and Juliet*, *The Lady of Shalott*, Leonardo DiCaprio drifting so handsomely down through the waters in *Titanic*—even Jesus lived fast and died young.

Eloi, eloi, lma sabbacthani—My God, My God, why have you forsaken me?[25] Don't yield to this temptation. Emily should be here, right here, right now. She should be with us, laughing or cussing, in mismatched socks and a duct tape ball gown. Emily should be living her way into all the fine and funny days that stretched before her. Her life was going to be messy and interesting, with friends and travels, kids and causes. She had more paintings in her, and if I may say so, our world has been diminished by what we now will never see.

I make this point especially for those of you who are around Emily's age: You may someday meet the dragon. Perhaps, you have already met him—he gets around. I must tell you this as bluntly as I can: Fight. Fight hard. Don't you dare declare, by letting go of any part

25. Matt 27:46

of your life, let alone the whole of it, that what Emily lost wasn't worth having in the first place. Life was—and remains—a gift. If you would pay tribute to Emily, do so by valuing your life and living it all the way to a ripe and righteous old age. Learn from the wrong weapons Emily chose with which to fight the dragon.

Emily is gone.

The dragon called depression got hold of her, and Emily's life ended. But the dragon could not win by death. After all, as our Buddhist friends remind us, everybody dies.

No, the dragon seeks to terminate not life, but love. And Emily may have run out of time or out of strength, but she was never out of love. She lived in love; she died in love. And our presence here with our breaking hearts is proof; we love Emily still. We love Emily. And we always will.

So be angry if you have to, for anger is the voice of love frustrated. And let your tears roll down if that same love provokes your grief. By your friendship, you have earned the right to be angry with Emily, and you have the right to cry for her. And let your heart break if it must. Faced with this death, what else can a good heart do? But if it breaks, let your heart break open. Let grief expand it into the only appropriate shrine, a heart courageous and capable of yet more generosity, more forgiveness, and more appreciation of the goodness of life. Faced with death—even this death—there is nothing else we can do and nothing else we need to do.

Join me, as you feel called, in a spirit of prayer or meditation:

Oh, merciful and tender God. We are grateful for the gift we were given in the life and person of Emily Ann.

We ask for blessings for Kerry, John, Andre, Grandma Maggie, and all of Emily's family. May they be held in love. May they find peace.

We ask blessings for her close friends. May they be held in love. May they find peace.

We ask blessings for this community. May it be held in love. May it find peace.

May God's tenderness be in our embrace of this family. May God's spirit inform our words and inspire our best and most attentive listening as we walk with this family, these friends, and this community along the hard and necessary road that lies ahead. May we someday come to know deeply, in our very bones, this truth, that Emily is safe, forgiven, and free.

Amen.

Remembering Emily: Friends' Remarks

Music

"Tide and the River" by Cindy Kallet

Pastoral Prayer

Let us take a moment in silence together to remember Emily. Taken all together, our memories conjure her. She is with us.

Now, whisper her name amongst the names of all those you have known and loved and lost.

We remember them. We will remember her.

Lord's Prayer (in unison)

Benediction

Fare thee well, our beautiful Emily. In faith and
Gratitude we turn again to life.
May the Lord bless and keep you
May the Lord make his face the shine upon you and be
Gracious to you. May the Lord life up his countenance upon
You, and give you peace.

[Perhaps a handout could be distributed with information for young people present regarding how to find effective help during this time of stress.—Ed.]

In Loving Memory of Charles Kenneth M.

April 21, 1978—July 13, 2001

REVEREND KAREN COVEY-MOORE

Prayer

Loving God,

We need to hear Your Word today. You have promised to comfort Your people. Open our hearts and minds to receive Your peace. Speak to our hearts this day. May the meditations of our hearts and the words of my mouth be acceptable in Your sight, my Lord and my Redeemer. Amen.

Let the arms of God enfold you.

"Look at him! God, the Master, comes in power, ready to go into action . . . Like a shepherd, he will care for his flock, gathering the lambs in his arms, Hugging them as he carries them, leading the nursing ewes to good pasture."[26]

One of the hardest things in the world to do is to face the death of one's own child. When that is compounded by the terrible reality that the child took his own life, it is almost unbearable. The questions that are raised are almost too hard to ask. And the answers are even harder to find.

Why did he do it? Why couldn't I stop it? How could God allow this?

The reality of suicide is brutal. The important thing for all of us to know is that suicide is the result of an illness. Societal issues, genetics, and personality traits all play a part. And just as with any other life-threatening condition, heart disease, cancer, etc., not everyone responds to treatment at the time of crisis. Some do—and some don't. We keep trying to find the perfect vaccine or preventive balm, but we are not there yet.

But suicide is not an unforgiveable sin!

There are six instances of suicide reported in the Hebrew Bible, e.g., Saul and Samson, etc., and none of those who died by their own choice are condemned for the way they died. Most were buried with honor and remembered for their accomplishments.

---

26. Peterson, *The Message*, Isa 40:10–11

The fact is, life on this earth is full of all kinds of suffering. The good news is that God loves us so much that he *chooses* to dwell among us and endure all the suffering of humanity! The *Cotton Patch Gospel* version of 2 Corinthians 5:19 reads, "God was in Christ, hugging the world to Himself . . . He did that by willingly going to the cross and enduring the awful pain and humility of the Cross." I believe that God understands the suffering of Charlie and all like him who suffer the anguish of depression. I believe that God understands the distress of grief and loss and the agony of living in a reality that is not pleasant or understandable.

One of the questions that arises in tragedy is, "Where was God?" or "Where is God?"

In Isaiah, we read, "Can a mother forget her infant, be without tenderness for the child of her womb? Even should she forget, I will not forget you. See, upon the palms of my hands I have written your name; your walls are ever before me."[27]

Jesus promised that he would never leave us. "And know that I am with you always, until the end of the world!"[28] "I will not leave you orphaned; I will come to you."[29]

Even though Charlie may not have been aware of it, Jesus was right there with him through all of his pain and suffering and as he took the final steps to end his life. Even though it was not a part of the plan that God intended, he was still there. And then Charlie was gathered into the arms of love, where his suffering ended, and fear and pain were no more.

And now, you are left to deal with the pain of grief and the sorrow of losing a precious son.

In Genesis, the story of Hagar addresses the agony of a mother who feels unable to save her son from certain death and does not know where to turn. Not once but twice, she finds herself in the wilderness crying. The first time, God *sees* her anguish and guides and strengthens her. The second time, God *hears* her cries and assures her that, while the future will not be what she had envisioned, it will, in fact, be ok.

In the same way, God sees your pain and hears your cries. The future is forever changed, but you are not alone. You, too, may feel like you are in a wilderness, and you will need to cry. But remember, God is with you! God sees and hears you and will never leave you.

27. Isa 49:15–16
28. Matt 28:20
29. John 14:18

The Message

I invite you today to allow those arms of love to carry you through this time of sorrow. Know that it is ok to acknowledge the pain of your loss. If you had not loved, it would not hurt. Treasure the gift of Charlie's life and give yourself permission to cry and mourn. Express your pain with tears. Talk to family and friends. There is power in telling the story.

It will get better.

You may always have a hole in your heart, but the pain will not be so intense.

You will heal.

God loves you dearly.

Rest assured that God is holding you and Charlie in the arms of his love.

Bibliography

Jordan, Clarence. *The Cotton Patch Gospel.* Macon, GA: Smyth & Helwys, 2004.
Peterson, Eugene H. *The Message: The Bible in Contemporary Language.* Colorado Springs, CO: NavPress, 2002.

Funeral for a Person Who Died by Suicide

REVEREND DAYMOND DUCK

After opening remarks, Reverend Duck gives the following advice to the family and friends.—Ed.

What advice can I give you?

First, look to God for strength. If you handle this death without God, you'll be leaving out your greatest and most important source of help. Be like the Psalmist, who said, "O Lord, my rock, my fortress, my deliverer. My God, my rock of refuge, my shield, the horn of my salvation, my stronghold!"[30] I want us to consider something that Jesus said, "I am the resurrection and the life: whoever believes in me, though he should die, will come to life."[31] *I am.* That's the name of God. He told Moses, "I am who I am."[32] *I am* means God exists. God is real. *I am* is a name that Jesus used dozens of times. But it's more than something he called himself. Because after he said *I am*, he raised Lazarus from the dead. Jesus also said, *he that believes in me, though he were dead, yet shall he live.* He that believes in me. J believed in Jesus. Though he were dead, yet shall he live. J will be raised from the dead. *The Living Bible* says, "Even though he dies like anyone else he shall live again."[33] Jesus made no exceptions. He placed no conditions on how we die. The time will come when J will literally be raised from the dead. God didn't approve of the way he died. But that didn't cancel out J's security as a believer. It didn't cancel out his good works, his hope beyond the grave, the promises God made to him. God won't go back on those promises. God's promises to us don't depend upon our good works. They depend on God's goodness, grace, mercy, righteousness and honesty. So trust God, and expect him to help you.

30. Ps 18:1
31. John 11:25
32. Exodus 3:14
33. Taylor, *The Living Bible*, John 11:25

Second, look to your family for strength. Love each other. Hug each other. Cry on each other's shoulders. Share the strength *you* have with others in your family. John said,

> Beloved, let us love one another because love is of God.; everyone who loves is begotten of God and has knowledge of God. The man without love has known nothing of God, for God is love. God's love was revealed in our midst in this way: he sent his only Son to the world that we might have life through him. Love, then, consists of this: not that we have loved God, but that he has loved us and has sent his Son as an offering for our sin. Beloved, if God has loved us so, we must have the same love for one another.[34]

Life is short. Love each other. If you don't, you're not doing the will of God.

Third, look to your friends for strength. Many people want to help you. Many have sent flowers, many have come to express sympathy and understanding. Let your church help you. We love you. We're praying for you. That's one of the reasons why the church is here, and our hearts go out to you.

Fourth, be thankful for the years that J lived. Lots of people don't live that long. Some who do are sick. Some can't get out and go. Some can't hold a job. J could. Be thankful for his life. He made a confession of faith in Jesus. He attended church. He lived right. Be thankful for that. Several church members have told me what a nice guy J was. He was good to people. Be thankful for that. He had a wonderful little boy. Be thankful for that. By the way, did you ever notice how J took care of his son? He brought him to MYF at Brazil last Sunday night. But he didn't just let him out of his vehicle and drive on. He got out and walked him inside the church. He came back and got him. But he didn't sit outside and wait on him. He came in and walked him out to his van. Be thankful for that. One of his last acts was to take his son to church. Don't tell me one mistake wipes that out. I'll never believe it.

Fifth, we didn't want to give J up, the Bible teaches that some nuggets of good can come of moments like this. Paul said, *it's appointed unto man once to die.* Solomon said, *there is a time to be for every experience under heaven.* Both men were saying that death is a part of God's plan. We know that. So we need to make the most of our lives; to get our priorities straight. If J's death can cause just one person to live better, just one person to draw closer to God, just one person to accept Jesus Christ, then his death wasn't in vain.

---

34. 1 John 4:7–11

Abe Vanderpoi asked a pastor's wife, "what put you in that wheelchair?"

She replied, "I had cancer in my leg and the doctors had to take it to save my life."

Losing her leg was awful, but losing her leg saved her life. Losing J was awful. But if losing J causes just one person to live better, good has come from it. Paul said, "We know that God makes all things work together for the good of those who have been called according to his decree."[35] When President Kennedy was assassinated, Governor John Connally and his wife were riding in the front of the limousine. Governor Connally said, *we could have died that day. As far as my wife and I are concerned, it brought into sharper focus what's really important in life.* President Kennedy's death was a bad thing, but good came from it. It made the Connally's understand the importance of life, the importance of family, the importance of loving each other, the importance of salvation, the importance of life beyond the grave.

Sixth, let J's death cause you to pull together. Families get separated, torn apart. The death of a loved one reminds us that we won't always be together. We need to make life better for each other while we can. Today, someone might say, *J made a mistake.* Yes, we all make mistakes. We can't help J, but we can help each other. We want God to overlook our mistakes. We should overlook each other's mistakes. Forgive each other. I believe J would want us to do that.

Seventh, let J's death increase your faith and worship. God is more than someone to go in crisis. He deserves more than our prayers when things are going bad. James said, "Draw close to God, and he will draw close to you."[36] That's an invitation to a relationship with God; an invitation to receive all of the benefits of an all-knowing, all-loving God. We need to be ready to go. James said,

> Come now, you who say, "Today or tomorrow we shall go to such and such a town, spend a year there, trade, and come off with a profit!" You have no idea what kind of life will be yours tomorrow. You are a vapor that appears briefly and vanishes. Instead of saying, "If the Lord wills it, we shall live to do this or that."[37]

We're not promised a tomorrow, a next week, or a next year. The best thing we can do while we're still alive is to make things right with God through Jesus. That's a good way to turn J's death into a victory.

35. Rom 8:28
36. Jas 4:8
37. Jas 4:13–15

Eighth, don't blame yourself. It's easy to say, *if I had been there, things would be different. If I had said this. If I had done that.* J was ___ years old. He was old enough to run his life. He did. He got confused. He made a bad decision. We've all done that. What good can we bring out of this? What good can God bring out of it?

I want to close with a story from *Difficult Funeral Services* by James L. Christensen. A famous man terminated his life. Everyone was shocked. His family planned a short funeral, a prayer, a little music, and some Scripture. That's all. The service was almost over when the man's daughter stood up.

She said, "My dad was a good man. He was good to us. He was good to a lot of people. We should never forget that. It's true that dad got depressed, true that he lost his zeal for life. But I want to ask you to remember his good qualities. I want to ask you to pray for his family. I want to ask you for your understanding and love. And I want to ask God for His mercy for my dad. But remember, please, dad was a good man."

We've gathered here to honor the memory of J. I ask you to remember the good things, his childhood, his teen years, the happy times, the good things he said, the good things he did. Keep those pictures. Remember the good things.

This would be a good place to insert the good things in J's life.—Ed.

Finally, we ask God for mercy and grace for J God's mercy and grace are real. The Bible says, his mercy triumphs over judgment.[38] It says his grace is free to J and to each one of us.

Prayer

Almighty God, we believe that you are always with us. We give you our worship and praise. Even during this trying time, we worship you because you are worthy of our worship. Forgive our sins. As we gather in your presence, we ask your mercy for J. We ask for thy forgiving love for J. We ask for thy marvelous grace to keep working in his life. And God we ask you to comfort his family. You promised that if we would come to you, we would not be turned away. Forgive us for ignoring you. Bless J's family. Give them strength and understanding. Speak to all of us of eternal things. Challenge

---

38. Jas 2:13

our hearts to serve thee. Thank you for being good to us. Thank you for J's life. Minister unto his needs, and unto the needs of his family.

Bibliography

Christensen, James L. *Difficult Funeral Services.* Old Tappan, NJ: F.H. Revell, 1985.
Taylor, Kenneth Nathaniel. *The Living Bible, Paraphrased.* Wheaton, IL: Tyndale House; Distributed by Doubleday, 1971.

A Sermon for a Death by Suicide
Life is a Mystery

Reverend Charles T. Rubey

One of the questions that grip survivors of a suicide is, *why?* Survivors wonder why someone they loved and knew in this world would take their life. That's what makes suicide different from other forms of death. If a person died from heart disease or an automobile accident or drowned, people would know why that person died. When death occurs by suicide, the looming question is, *why?* What did I do or not do that brought this loved one of mine to suicide?

We, as Christian people, are asked to grapple and wrestle with mystery. This God of ours is a mysterious God, and unless we are willing to wrestle and grapple with mystery, we do not have an adequate or proper attitude or understanding of God. Our God is a God of mystery. We don't understand many of the things that happen in our world. We don't understand child abuse or cancer or mental illness or suicide. The reason why these things plague our world is a mystery. The challenge that you and I have as Christian people is to maintain an abiding and deep trust and faith in an all-wise, all-provident God while all around us unexplainable events go on.

Our God is all-wise, all-provident, and we, as humans, have the right to question the whys and wherefores of our world. But underlying all of this is the fact that our God is a God of mystery. After saying the words of consecration over the bread and wine the priest declares, *let us proclaim the mysteries of our faith.* To me, the emphasis is on the mystery of faith because it is mysterious. There are no answers, and that is one of the reasons that we come to God at a time like this, completely at the mercy of this mysterious God of ours.

When the priest adds a few drops of water to the wine he prays, *by the mystery of this water and wine.* To me, the emphasis is on the mystery because God is mysterious. Unless we are willing to grapple and wrestle with mystery, we will always fall short in our expectation and belief in God.

Faith in God means that we don't always understand, that we take somewhat of a blind leap in this journey and that we grasp on to God because without God, where do we go? Our God in Jesus has the words of everlasting life. Does our faith comfort? Yes. Does it bring consolation? Yes. And it does add a dimension in a world that cannot be explained rationally. In a rational way, how does one explain the phenomenon of suicide? It defies explanation. It transcends explanation, and yet, somehow this is part of God's plan. Does God cause suicide? No. Why does God allow it? Who knows? The challenge we have is to maintain a deep and abiding faith in an all-wise, all-provident God and continue to adore this God and praise this God in light and in spite of what goes on to the world around us.

We pray that this loved one is at peace and for this, we are grateful. Peace evaded ___ in life, and that is the reason he/she took his/her life. But our prayers are not answered because we as survivors—those who loved this person so much in life—are gripped now by the pain of permanent loss. How does this fits into God's plan? We don't know. Why? We don't know. Our God is a God of mystery. Our God transcends rational explanation.

In other scriptural passages, Jesus invites us to "come to me, all who are weary and find life burdensome, and I will refresh you."[39] Does this passage mean that if we go to Jesus we will be comforted and consoled? Not always. Our consolation and our comfort at times are tossed about in the storm of life. We don't find rest.

In another scriptural passage Jesus said that, "my yoke is easy and my burden is light."[40] Grieving a death from a suicide is not easy nor is the burden light. Yes, faith can console or to comfort. But it is also meant to be an affirming assent to an all-wise, all-provident, all-*mysterious* God.

As we commend our loved one to the Lord, let us be consoled and comforted knowing that ___ is cloaked and wrapped in the mysterious presence of the God of peace and the God of consolation.

39. Matt 11:28
40. Matt 11:30

Chapter Four

Perspectives

ᵔ

The Church and Suicide
Then and Now

Reverend James T. Clemons

Every human society whose members' behavior is detailed in extant records has included individuals who by their own decision and agency forfeited their own lives. Depending on the circumstances of their deaths, their fellows either memorialized them as heroes or condemned them as misguided or weak or evil persons.[1]

T his opening statement of Clebsch's introduction to his important work succinctly summarizes the entire history of the ethical issues inherent in discussions regarding suicide.

> Historical perspective is essential to achieving a clear understanding of one's own approach to the Bible. Much of what passes for new interpretation is really quite old. Errors of fact, mistakes of judgment, limitations of vision, and the need for charity are often forgotten. When individuals or communities use the Bible for

1. Clebsch, *Suicide*, vii

personal faith and ethical decision making today, their conclusions will always be short-sighted without a careful look at the history of exegesis.[2]

Clebsch goes on to say, "in Asian societies, the deed has tended to be noncontroversial and rather honorable than despicable."[3] But ask anyone in the Western world what he or she first heard about suicide, and the answer is almost certainly to be, *if you take your life, you go to Hell.* This centuries-old teaching of the Christian faith became the basis for severe *legal* prohibition and oppressive *social* consequences. It has been generally assumed that this condemnation was based on one of the Ten Commandments and, to a lesser extent, the New Testament.

Having grown up with that common teaching, my later studies of the Bible raised questions as to what those biblical texts actually said about suicide, what they meant in their original contexts, and how they were interpreted through the ages to reach the unquestioned authority they came to have. I was further intrigued when I learned that leaders in psychiatry and sociology believed such teachings contributed to individual mental illness and to societal barriers to prevention.

While teaching a class for doctoral students at Wesley Theological Seminary, I decided to lecture on suicide and the Bible, expecting to find ample resources available. I was not expecting to find that there was not, or ever had been, a detailed study of that subject, and that there was no discussion of the term in current bible dictionaries and encyclopedias.

Even more surprising to learn was that leading biblical commentators, in their exegesis of the several accounts of those who had taken their own lives, never mentioned that the death was, in fact, a suicide. No comment as to what it meant for the author's intent, nothing about the society in which it first occurred, never a word on the theological dimensions of the human act nor its meaning for the faithful community that has continued to consider the accounts as part of Scripture through all the centuries since.

The best treatment of that nature is by Bruce C. Birch in his commentary on the death of Saul which appeared in *The New Interpreter's Bible* in 1998.[4] It is an excellent, straightforward interpretation of Saul as a suicide followed by a most helpful reflection on the meaning of the passage for preachers.

2. Clemons, *What Does the Bible*, 75–76

3. Clebsch, *Suicide*

4. Birch, *The New Interpreter's Bible*, 11971198

It was that unfortunate vacuum among earlier commentators that called me to write *What Does the Bible Say About Suicide?*, which first appeared in 1990. My initial task was to define suicide in a way that would encompass all of the specific accounts and related texts necessary to gain a full understanding of what the Bible really says and does not say. The six texts in Hebrew Scripture and the two references to Judas in the New Testament are listed in chapter 4, "References in Religious Writings." The best known individuals are Saul, his armor-bearer, and Judas. Most would be reluctant to include Samson, but the entire account passage related to his death is worthy of study. Least known are the deaths of Abimelech, Ahithophel, and Zimri. Each is discussed in my aforementioned book, together with more than seventy other biblical texts that have been used either to condemn or to condone suicide.

My conclusion was that in none of these texts was there any explicit condemnation of the act itself. This view is generally accepted by biblical scholars today. Nor does a survey of Christian writings of the first few centuries reveal such a condemnation.

It was not until 438 that Augustine, one of the greatest of Christian theologians and preachers, argued in his *City of God* that the commandment "you shall not kill" meant "you shall not kill yourself." There was no circumstance in which self-chosen death was acceptable. To commit the greater sin of suicide in order to avoid a lesser sin, whether intense suffering, rape, torture, or imminent death at the hands of one's enemies, was unacceptable for the Christian. What Augustine failed to note is that all of the six accounts are found in the earliest portions of Scripture, and that when later biblical writers referred to them, not one suggested that any of those who had taken their lives had broken the commandment.

With his power as a thinker, preacher, and church leader, Augustine won the day, and his argument that there was no forgiveness was reinforced over the centuries by ecumenical councils of the Church. Prohibitions against those who had committed this sin became more severe. There would be no last rites and no burials in consecrated cemeteries. At one point, some saints who had taken their lives were removed from that sacred status.

In the thirteenth century, Thomas Aquinas wrote the most influential summary of Christian theology, *Summa Theologicae*. It was in the format of a series of questions and answers, a catechism touching every aspect of the faith. When he came to ask, *what is man*, he included a statement on the end of human life, in which he accepted Augustine's basic position, and also reinforced it with additional arguments drawn from Greek philosophy and the notion of Natural Law.

Thereafter, the condemnation of suicide was beyond question, and in nations where Christianity was dominant, it was seen as both a sin and a crime. This led to the shameful social acts of dragging the bodies of those who had committed the sin through the streets to receive horrible abuse from the community before being exposed on a pole at the edge of town or buried with a stake through the heart. In some instances, families could not inherit anything belonging to the deceased. Their possessions went to the king or queen, who had lost a taxpayer and a servant in time of war. In England, those who attempted suicide and failed to do so had thereby committed a felony and could be arrested, brought to trial, and, if found guilty, condemned to die.

The late Middle Ages brought the intellectual Renaissance, which ushered in a new era of freedom that led common people to take a fresh look at the world, religion, and their human capabilities. Nothing, neither state nor church, was beyond open challenge. Rational thought focused on what was best for humans here and now. Individuals could think for themselves without having their entire lives decided by someone else's rules, be it a church that focused on otherworldliness or state-controlled elite rulers intolerant of the lower classes.

John Donne, an English cleric well known for his poetry, was head of St. Paul's Church in seventeenth century London. He wrote a book titled *Biathanatos*, in which he argued that those who took their lives should not be condemned. His arguments were based in large part on the New Testament[5], with a few references to Hebrew Scripture.[6] He did not allow his book to be published in his lifetime, but it first appeared in 1647.

The eighteenth century was that period of Western history commonly referred to as the Age of Reason, which brought further challenges to established beliefs. It was in this context that the thirteen colonies challenged England for their freedom, but there was little change in the prevailing views with regard to suicide.

Only in the late nineteenth century did suicide receive scientific study. Emile Durkheim was a leader among a group in France who were convinced

5. Matt 26:29, John 10:1118, 12:25, 13:37, 1:13, Rom 9:3, 2 Cor 12:15, Gal 4:15, Phil 1:20, John 3:16

6. Exod 32;32, Job 7:15, 21, Jonah 1:12, 4:15

that society itself had much to do with the way individuals behave. These men were founders of what is now recognized as sociology, but they were not accepted by the scientific community. What they needed was a study to prove their thesis.

It fell to Durkheim to undertake the task. He recognized that the act of suicide was everywhere considered a sin and a crime, committed solely by individuals who alone made that choice, although some allowance was made for mental incompetency. If he could show that such an individual act was influenced in large part by society, he could demonstrate that the new field of study had a scientific basis.

At the core of sociology, then as now, were statistics. Durkheim went to the morgues in Paris and collected an immense volume of data on those who had taken their lives, including gender, age, and method of suicide. He interpreted the data and concluded that there were four basic ways in which society influenced such individual behavior. Two of those are well known today. One was anomie, or the sense of profound loneliness, of having lost one's roots and purpose in life. This condition is often prevalent among people who move to a large, crowded environment, such as a city like Paris, after growing up in a small community with family and friends that gave meaning and purpose to one's existence. Today, the displacement of people by war, famine, natural disasters, or economics, as with much current immigration in the United States, is a major concern of the United Nations.

Another social influence identified by Durkheim as bearing on those who took their lives was altruism, the giving of one's life for the welfare of someone else, as exemplified by the biblical Jonah. Durkheim's work, *Le Suicide*, accomplished his goal and is generally considered to mark the beginning of sociology. A specific result was that his arguments, although both his methodology and conclusions are questioned today, removed a heavy burden that for so long had fallen entirely on the individual, making it easier to condone the act, though not to encourage it.

Clebsch's reference to the fact that some societies revere the self-chosen death of some heroes is apparent in the United States. We give Medals of Honor to some military personnel and others who are recognized in public ceremonies where clergy are often asked to participate.

Today, suicidology is itself a recognized field of study, separate from but closely related to sociology. The American Association of Suicidology is a research organization with headquarters in Washington, DC, and the

International Association of Suicidology meets annually in different cities around the globe with hundreds of countries represented.

The second significant factor that brought major change in attitudes toward suicide came with the work of Sigmund Freud and the beginnings of psychiatry in the 1920s and 1930s. Freud argued that the mind played tricks on individuals, causing them to act in ways over which they had no control. This theory was widely received, although many within Christian traditions rejected psychiatry as promoting a denial of faith, or at least criticizing Church teachings.

There is now a mutual respect between the two professions, benefiting both groups. Perhaps the most important reason for this relationship was the beginning of the Clinical Pastoral Training movement, begun primarily by Antoine Boison in mental hospitals and Russell Dicks in general hospitals.. Boston University was the early leader in developing this area of ministerial training. Many seminaries and schools of theology now require at least one course in pastoral care and offer supervised experiences in pastoral counseling based on psychiatric understandings of human behavior.

[This historical perspective can provide important information for those who are called upon to preach the suicide funeral and, in many instances, to continue their ministry after the funeral, a topic discussed in the final chapter here.—Ed.]

Bibliography

Birch, Bruce C., R. E. Clements, Peter D. Quinn-Miscall, Robert B. Coote, Dennis L. Olson, Kathleen A. Robertson. Farmer, and Thomas B. Dozeman. *The New Interpreter's Bible: A Commentary in Twelve Volumes.* Vol. 2. Nashville, TN: Abingdon, 1998. 1197–1198.

Clebsch, William A. *Suicide: "Biathanatos" Transcribed and Edited for Modern Readers.* Edited by John Donne. Chico, CA: Scholars Pr., 1983.

Clemons, James T. *What Does the Bible Say about Suicide?* Minneapolis: Fortress Press, 1990.

Suicide Through the Ages

RABBI EARL A. GROLLMAN

Natural death has its share of profound emotional overtones. One of the most complicated situations is a suicide. Yet, people have been killing themselves since the beginning of recorded time. How have attitudes toward suicide evolved through the generations?

Let us peruse the history of chronicled events to understand its meaning today from psychological, sociological, and legal perspectives. In this article, we focus on Judeo-Christian traditions. But first, we must learn from other earlier cultures and traditions. It must be noted that we have much to learn from other cultures and religions as well.

Egyptian, Greek, Roman, and Later Cultures

The First Egyptian Period (Seventh to Tenth Dynasty, 2000 BCE) documents the life of a man who was filled with unendurable pain and suffering. He did not consider suicide a violation of his spiritual or legal code.

Stoicism (the school of philosophy about 300 BCE) asserted that when circumstances were no longer tolerable, one could voluntarily withdraw from life by taking that life.

Epicureans (according to the founder, Epicurus, born in 341 BCE) concluded that when the attainment of pleasure was no longer possible, death is the viable alternative.

There were the dissenters. *Plato* (427 BCE–347 BCE) believed that people, even while suffering from extreme injustice, must find the courage to endure.

First Centuries —Judaism and Christianity

Judaism

"God looked at everything he had made, and found it very good."[7] With almost the first words of Genesis, there is the assertion that *life is good* and

7. Gen 1:31

that each person should treasure it and never despair of its possibilities, for behind it is God.

Despite a religious emphasis on the sanctity of life, the Holy Scriptures contain but six reference to suicide. In each case, there are extenuating circumstances, such as the fear of being taken captive or the possibility of suffering humiliation or unbearable pain. Saul, the first king of Israel (1020 BCE), fell upon his own sword to prevent being mocked and tortured by the Philistines.

When capture by the Romans became a certainty, a Jewish community in 73 CE committed mass suicide in the fortress of Masada.

There is an interesting twist with the great Jewish historian Flavius Josephus (37–200 CE). In his earlier works, Josephus extolled King Saul for his suicidal action and all the martyrs, for "better that they should die . . . thus gaining commendation and lasting names."[8]

Later, Josephus reversed this position. Conditions changed. An increasing number of suicides were recorded. The rise was partly due to the growing Greco-Roman influences and the rise in spiritual and social crises. Now that the suicidal act had become more frequent, a condemnatory tone was introduced. The ancient Israelites were intensely concerned for the survival of their tiny nomadic tribe. The suicide of even one Hebrew was a threat to tribal continuity.

As a result, suicides were buried outside the cemeteries at crossroads as a sign of disgrace. There were even instances of indignities practiced upon the corpse—the body was dragged through the streets, and the dead person was left for preying birds to consume.

Early Christianity

When Christianity came into being, suicide was very common in Greece and Rome. The early Christians accepted the prevailing attitude of their era, particularly when persecution made life unbearable. To escape the Roman torture, many took their lives, preferring to be martyrs to their cause.

The Apostles did not denounce self-execution. The New Testament touched on this question only indirectly in the report of Judas's death. For several centuries, the leaders of the church did not condemn this widespread practice.

---

8. Josephus 14:4

The year 313 CE is noteworthy. The Christian maltreatment had ended. Christianity was now the official religion of Rome. They were in charge.

Until Augustine (354–430 CE) denounced suicide as a sin, there was no official Church position against it. After deliberating at great length whether a suicide death could be condoned in the case of a woman whose honor was in danger, Augustine declared that suicide is an act which precluded the possibility of repentance, and it is a form of homicide and this is a violation of the Decalogue article 'Thou shalt not kill.'[9]

The Second Council of Churches expressed the earliest organizational disapproval of suicide in 533 CE. Suicide was regarded as the most serious and heinous of all transgressions.

The Council of Hereford in 672 CE withheld burial rites to those who took their lives. In 1284 CE, the Synod of Nimes refused suicides in holy ground.

A further elaboration of the Augustinian concept was cited by Thomas Aquinas (1224–1274 CE). He opposed suicide on the basis of three postulates, it was against the natural inclinations of preservation of life and charity toward the self, it was a trespass against the community, and it was a trespass against God, who had given life to humanity.

Suicide and the Courts

Theological restrictions were translated into both criminal and civil laws. Early English practice penalized survivors by confiscating their property. In the sixteenth century, a person who persuaded another to assist in one's suicide was guilty of murder. The doctrine of "blameworthy intent" equated suicide with homicide. A parliamentary act directed that burying a suicide could take place in church cemeteries but without religious ceremony and only between nine pm and midnight.

Suicide was a felony in England and many other countries. The punishment for an attempted suicide was imprisonment. Sir William Blackstone, the distinguished English jurist (1723–1780), considered suicide to be a double curse both against the king and God. Statutes were enacted against suicide attempts and the survivors.

These laws did not prevent the increase of suicides. The courts learned that they had no power in stopping people from taking their lives. It was not until 1961 that the British Parliament enacted a bill abolishing the

9. Augustine, *City of God*, Book 1, Chapter 17

criminality of suicides. Both in Canada and the United States, laws were finally decreed that suicide was not an indictable offense.

While suicide was a taboo subject with stiff sentences for the suicidal person who tried but failed, there were noted personalities who differed. The Jewish sage Yoseph Karo (1488–1575) approached the subject from the standpoint of mental illness, that he had done the deed unwittingly. John Donne (1572–1632), the dean of St. Paul's Cathedral and renowned poet, had himself as a youth contemplated taking his life. In his book *Biathanatos*, he later made a plea for charity and acceptance.

His position was echoed by many secular writers and philosophers. Hume, Montesquieu, Voltaire, and Rousseau wrote essays defending suicide under certain conditions and argued for greater understanding and freedom against ecclesiastical authorities.

Today, many disciplines view suicide not from the legal and theological perspectives, but rather for psychological and sociological implications. Religious approaches are counterbalanced with the perspectives of the social sciences. Increasingly, suicide is recognized not only as a profound religious question but also as a major medical problem.

For example, the late Richard Cardinal Cushing issued an interpretation of Canon 1240, stating that the Church forbids Christian burial to suicides, but only if they were in full possession of their faculties at the time of the crime.

Prominent clergyman Dr. Norman Vincent Peale wrote in *The Healing of Sorrow*, "For we do not know how many battles have been fought and won before he or she loses that one particular battle. And is it fair that all the good acts and impulses of such a person should be forgotten or blotted out by the final act? I think our reaction should be one of love and pity, not condemnation."[10]

No one is suggesting that suicide is desirable or commendable. Just as jurists have revoked anti-suicide statutes, so have many in the religious realm been re-evaluating their attitudes. Our goal is to understand the complexities of our clients. For prevention, we could review the recent studies to broaden our views, especially in relation to mental health. Consider these questions, what can we do for meaningful interventions, and in postvention, what compassionate support can we offer to the survivors?

As Bishop John Robinson explains, "Truth finds expression in different ages."

10. Peale, *The Healing of Sorrow*

References

Josephus, Flavius. *The Works of Flavius Josephus, the Learned and Authentic Jewish Historian.* Translated by William Whiston. London: Henry G. Bohn, 1852.

Peale, Norman Vincent. *The Healing of Sorrow.* Pawling, NY: Inspirational Book Service; Distributed to the Book Trade by Doubleday, Garden City, N.Y., 1966.

Cultivating Connection, Compassion, and Confidence in Goodness
While Healing After Suicide

Bhikshuni Thubten Chodron

While in retreat in 2006, I received an invitation to speak at a conference for survivors of suicide. These were some of my preliminary thoughts, but when the time came, I left the paper aside and spoke as one human being to another. For the audio file of the talk, go to http://www.thubtenchodron.org/ DeathAndDying/loss_of_a_loved_one_to_suicide.html.

It is my honor and privilege to be able to share some reflections with such an esteemed audience, a group of people who genuinely and sincerely care about other living beings. That care and affection for others—that feeling of being connected—is an important element in living a meaningful life. Related to that is feeling that there is something basically good and pure about us human beings, despite our suffering and anger. We are aware that we have special potential simply because we have a mind/heart, that our life is not one condemned to alienation, self-hatred, guilt, and resentment. In Buddhist language, we call that "Buddha nature" or "Buddha potential"— the completely clear nature of our mind/heart that is the foundation upon which we can develop amazing qualities, such as impartial love and compassion for all living beings and a wisdom that knows the ultimate reality of all existence.

I would like to talk more about these two, the feeling of connection with others that leads to compassion and the awareness of our inner goodness or *potential for enlightenment*, because they are interconnected with both suicide and healing after the suicide of a dear one.

First, let's investigate how they are related to suicide itself. Suicide often stems from depression. While in some cases depression may be due to chemical imbalance or interfering forces, nevertheless, some prominent thoughts ransack the mind, provoking some people to consider suicide as a way to alleviate their misery. These are thoughts such as, *my life is useless, there is no hope for happiness in my life*, and *I am not worthwhile enough to live.* On what grounds does the thought *my life is useless* arise? Its basis is not feeling connected with others or with one's environment. We can see that, while such a thought may exist, its contents are unrealistic, for, in fact, we are deeply connected with and related to all living beings. We depend on each other throughout our lives.

How can we oppose this unrealistic view? The Buddha laid out a series of meditations designed to develop love and compassion. Just telling ourselves to feel loving, loved, or connected does not work. We have to actively train our mind/heart to look at life from a different perspective. When this is done, positive emotions will naturally arise.

The foundation of this training is seeing that ourselves and others are totally equal in wanting happiness and wishing to avoid any and all kinds of suffering. We contemplate this deeply and repeatedly, not just saying the words at an intellectual level but bringing them into our heart. In this way, we train our mind/heart so that every time we see any living being—no matter who they are, whether we like them or not—our spontaneous awareness is, *this living being is exactly like me. The most important thing for him or her is happiness and avoiding suffering. Recognizing this, I understand something very important, very intimate about others. We are indeed interconnected.* Even if we've never met someone, we know that this is how that person feels. Even animals and insects have happiness and the eradication of misery as the most important purposes of their lives. When we continually train our mind to see everyone in this way, we no longer feel alienated. Instead, we feel and know that we are enmeshed in this interconnected body of living beings. We belong; we understand others, and they can understand us. Our actions affect them; we are not isolated, walled-in units but part of the whole of living beings throughout this universe. Our problems are not unique and hopeless. We can reach out to help other beings and to contribute to their happiness, even in small ways that become deeply meaningful. We allow ourselves to receive others' affection and aid. Our life has purpose.

Not only does our life have meaning, but we deserve to live. We are a worthy living being. Why? Because our basic nature is something good, something pure. Sure, we have all sorts of disturbing emotions, but they are not us. They are mental events, things that arise, pass though, and leave our minds. We are not our thoughts and feelings. They are not us. When we sit in meditation and are mindful of our thoughts and feelings, this becomes quite evident. Underneath them is the basic clear and knowing nature of mind/heart, which is free from all thoughts and emotions. On a deeper level, our nature is like the pure and clear open sky. Clouds may pass through it, but the sky and the clouds are not the same nature. Even when the clouds are present, the pure and open sky still exists; it can never be destroyed. Similarly, the nature of our mind is not inherently defiled; the disturbing attitudes and emotions are adventitious.

Not only are disturbing emotions and thoughts transient, they are also distorted. They are not accurate views of what is happening nor beneficial responses to it. Instead of believing everything we think and feel, we investigate our thoughts and feelings to discern if they are accurate and beneficial. Should we discover they aren't, we apply antidotes by training our mind to view situations in a different way, one that is more accurate and beneficial. As we do this, we discover that our *take* on life changes; we discover our inner goodness. We are worthwhile and have been all along; only now, we see it.

How do these points, connection, compassion, and potential for enlightenment, relate to those healing from suicide? First, compassion for ourselves and for the one who completed suicide is called for. It's easy to feel guilty and blame ourselves for another's suicide. It's easy to be angry at them for making us suffer. It's easy to sink into our grief at losing a loved one and become immersed in self-pity. But these emotions are like clouds in the sky of the spacious purity of our mind/heart. They are not us; we are not them. They arise and pass through our minds. There is no benefit to grasping onto disturbing emotions and imbuing them with a reality that they don't have.

In addition, all those feelings, guilt, anger, resentment, self-pity, are functions of our self-preoccupied attitude. It is this self-centeredness that has kept us trapped in misery from time without beginning. Not only is self-centeredness not beneficial for our own or others' happiness, but it's also not realistic. There are infinite living beings. Let's place our own pain within the perspective of all the varied experiences that living beings have at this moment.

That doesn't mean we're bad if we temporarily get stuck in disturbing emotions. Let's not add another layer of delusion on top of what we're already feeling by telling ourselves that we're selfish and wrong for being depressed or self-preoccupied. Rather, since those are unrealistic and unbeneficial feelings, let's ask ourselves, *what are more realistic and suitable ones? How do I cultivate them?*

Here is where compassion for ourselves comes in. Compassion is not self-pity. Rather, it acknowledges our pain and confusion, wishes ourselves to be free from them, and then moves on.

What does it move on to? What do we consciously cultivate? A heart that cares about others. The feeling of connection and compassion we had for the dear one who completed suicide is for one living being. There are infinite living beings throughout the universe. What would happen if we were to take down the walls of obsessive clinging to one person and open our hearts to loving all beings simply because they exist? We can share the love we had for one person with many others, increasing our capacity to give and receive love while we do so.

Several years ago, I was asked to preside over a memorial service for a man in his thirties who had died of cancer. When his wife spoke at the service, she was radiant.

She said, "John, I'm going to take all that love you gave me, all the love we shared together into my heart. And then, because it's not something that can ever diminish, I'm going to spread it out from my heart to everyone I encounter."

I was tremendously moved by what she said, and I'm sure her husband would have been as well.

Grief after the death of a loved one is not about missing them in the present as much as realizing that our image of the future—a future which had included them—needs to be changed. In other words, we're not mourning the past; we're mourning the future. But the future never was, was it? It was only our conception, so why cling on to something that was never there? Instead, let's rejoice that we knew this person for as long as we did. How wonderful that we were able to share and to learn from each other for as long as we did. Everything is transient; and we were so fortunate to have them in our lives and to love them and be loved by them for as long as we did.

What an incredible way to heal from the death of a loved one, to rejoice at the time we had together instead of to mourn for the future that never was and will never be. How meaningful it is to share the love we have for one person by opening our hearts to all others and giving that love to them. This enables us to have love and compassion for our loved one, wherever the continuity of *what they were* is. We send them off with love, wishing them the best, knowing that they have the potential for enlightenment and praying that they will make use of their internal goodness in the future. We, too, have this potential for enlightenment, so let's access it within our own heart and mind and, having done so, live peacefully within ourselves and make a positive contribution to the well-being of others.

Many of you survivors have used compassion for others to help you heal after the death of your loved one. Your compassion led you to organize this conference, to set forth initiatives for government programs and policies, to begin suicide prevention programs, support groups, and so on. I commend your compassionate efforts to help others and know that you and they will experience the beneficial results of that. Many of you are still fresh in your grief. You are not ready to do this yet. But trust in yourself that you will reach the point where you can transform your experience into something that activates you to help others.

Many of you may be curious about the role of meditation in developing these perspectives. There are many forms of meditation. One type that is useful is called *mindfulness meditation*. Here, we may focus on our breath, physical sensations, feelings, mind, or thoughts and simply observe them, letting them arise and pass without clinging on to them. By doing this, we come to see these as simply events, nothing permanent to get attached to or hold on to. Our mind relaxes. We also begin to see that these mental and physical events are not us; we see that there is no solid *I* or *mine* to control or possess all these events. This releases the stress in our minds.

A second type of meditation is what is called *analytic* or *checking* meditation. Here, a genre of teachings entitled *mind training* or *thought transformation* is very effective. The thought transformation teachings instruct us how to actively develop a feeling of connection equally for all living beings. They show the method to cultivate love, compassion, joy, and equanimity. They also teach how to transform adverse circumstances into the path to enlightenment—a very useful skill. Let me recommend a few books I have written on this topic, *Transforming Adversity into Joy and Courage, Advice from a Spiritual Friend, Thought Training like Rays of the Sun, Mindfulness in Plain English*, and *The Miracle of Mindfulness*. You may also want to attend talks given by qualified Buddhist teachers.

Healing After Suicide

BHIKSHUNI THUBTEN CHODRON

"My son, John, who I loved dearly, shot himself on March 23rd five years ago, when he was twenty-seven years old."

"On May 4th, 2001, my treasured daughter, Susan, died. She hung herself."

Around the room we went, introducing ourselves, each parent saying their own name and introducing their child who died. I was in a break-out group for parents who had lost their adult children to suicide at the 18th Annual Healing After Suicide Conference in Seattle in April, 2006, which was organized by SPAN (Suicide Prevention Action Network) and AAS (American Association of Suicidology). The pain in the room was palpable, but there was also a feeling of close community. Finally, people who had experienced a pain that is rarely spoken of in society, the pain of losing a loved one to suicide, could talk freely to other survivors of suicide who understood what they were going through.

I'd been asked to give the luncheon address as well as to participate in a panel entitled "Suicide: The Challenge to a Survivor's Faith and Spirituality and Faith Community Response" at this conference. It was a good thing that my meditation practice had accustomed me to accepting pain, for there was plenty of it here, but there were also a warmth and love that are not found at national conferences on other issues. People reached out to strangers because their experiences were not strange.

In the hotel foyer were quilts on the wall, each panel with the face of someone's loved one who had died by suicide. I looked at the faces, young, old, middle-aged, black, white, Asian. Each of these people has a story, and each left a story of love and of grief behind as their loved ones struggle to understand and accept.

To prepare to speak at this conference, I'd asked the participants of a retreat I was leading, *who has lost a dear one to suicide?* I was amazed how many hands went up. In reading up on the topic, I was startled to learn that older, white men had the highest suicide rate of all groups. Among teenagers who try to kill themselves, more are girls. However, boys are more successful in completing it. Certainly, we need more discussion in the media and public forums about how to prevent suicide and how to diagnose and treat depression. Also, we need to discuss what happens to the family and friends of those who chose to end their lives. What are the survivors' needs and experiences?

Several survivors at the conference said that they were stigmatized by their friends or communities because of a suicide occurring in their family. I guess I'm naïve. I'd never thought that others would close their hearts to friends who were grieving a suicide. I wonder if it was a case of closed hearts or one of people's own discomfort about death, or perhaps they wanted to help but didn't know how.

Some people spoke of friends who *said the wrong thing*—that was not helpful to their grieving process. *Uh oh*, I thought, *what if I unintentionally do this during my lunchtime talk?* But my fear subsided in the wake of their openness about their feelings. *If I don't "try to help," but am just myself,* I thought, *it'll be okay, just one human being to another.*

After the talk, several people came up to thank me for the *breath of fresh air* that talking about compassion brought. I left the conference with great gratitude for all that these courageous survivors had given me by being so open, transparent, and supportive of each other. I especially admire all those in SPAN and AAS who are survivors of suicide and who have transformed their grief into beneficial action for others. My appreciation has grown for the need to expand diagnosis and treatment of depression and bipolar disorder, to educate the public about the importance of suicide prevention, and to care for those who are grieving the loss of a dear one.

The comment of one father touched me deeply. *When death comes,* he said, *make sure you're really alive.* May we not drown in our complacency or live on automatic. May we cherish our lives and cherish the people around us.

Our Misconceptions About Suicide
To be Shared With Families

Father Ron Rolheiser

Sometimes, things need to be said, and said, and said until they don't need to be said any more. Margaret Atwood wrote that, and its truth is the reason why, each year, I write a column on suicide. We still have too many misconceptions about suicide.

I won't try to be original in this column but will simply try to re-state, as clearly as possible, what needs to be said over and over again. What are our misconceptions about suicide?

First, that suicide is an act of despair. Too common still is the belief that suicide is the ultimate act of despair—culpable and unforgivable. To die by suicide, it is too commonly believed, puts one under the judgment once pronounced on Judas Iscariot, better to not have been born. Until recently, victims of suicide were often not even buried in church cemeteries.

What is truer is that the propensity for suicide is, in most cases, an illness. We are made up of body and soul. Either can snap. We can die of cancer, high blood pressure, heart attacks, and aneurysms. These are physical sicknesses. But we can suffer these in the soul, as well. There are malignancies and aneurysms, too, of the heart, deadly wounds from which the soul cannot recover. In most cases, suicide, like any terminal illness, takes a person out of life against his or her will. The death is not freely chosen but is an illness, far from an act of free will. In most instances, suicide is a desperate attempt to end unendurable pain, much like a man who throws himself through a window because his clothing is on fire. That's a tragedy, not an act of despair.

Given the truth of this, we need to give up the notion that suicide puts a person outside the mercy of God. God's mercy is equal even to suicide. After the resurrection, we see how Christ, more than once, goes through locked doors and breathes forgiveness, love, and peace into hearts that are unable to open themselves because of fear and hurt. God's mercy and peace can go through walls that we can't. And, as we know, this side of heaven, sometimes all the love, stretched-out hands, and professional help in the world can no longer reach through to a heart paralyzed by fear and illness.

But when we are helpless, God is not. God's love can descend into hell itself, as we profess in our creed, and breathe peace and reconciliation inside wound, anger, and fear. God's hands are gentler than ours, God's compassion is wider than ours, and God's understanding infinitely surpasses our own. Our wounded loved ones who fall victim to suicide are safe in God's hands, safer by far than they are in the judgments that issue from our own limited understanding. God is not stymied by locked doors like we are.

In most cases, suicide is an illness, and when its victims wake on the other side, they are met by a gentle Christ who stands right inside of their huddled fear and says, *peace be with you!* As we see in the gospels, God can go through locked doors, breathe out peace in places where we cannot get in, and write straight with even the most crooked of lines.

Finally, too, there is a misunderstanding about suicide that expresses itself in second-guessing, *if only I had done more; if only I had been more attentive, this could have been prevented.* Rarely is this the case. Most of the time, we weren't there when our loved one died for the very reason that this person didn't want us to be there. He or she picked the time and place precisely with our absence in mind. Suicide is a disease that picks its victim precisely in such a way so as to exclude others and their attentiveness. That's part of the anatomy of the disease.

This, of course, may never be an excuse for insensitivity to those around us who are suffering from depression, but it's a healthy check against false guilt and anxious second-guessing. Many of us have stood at the bedside of someone who is dying and experienced a frustrating helplessness because there was nothing we could do to prevent our loved one from dying. That person died, despite our attentiveness, prayers, and efforts to be helpful. So, too, at least generally, with those who die of suicide, our love, attentiveness, and presence could not stop them from dying, despite our will and effort to the contrary.

The Christian response to suicide should not be horror, fear for the person's eternal salvation, and anxious self-examination about we did or didn't do. Suicide is, indeed, a terrible way to die, but we must understand it for what it is, a sickness, and stop being anxious about both the person's eternal salvation and our less-than-perfect response to his or her illness.

God redeems everything, and, in the end, all manner of being will be well, beyond even suicide.

Breaking Silence, Breaking Bread
To Be Shared With Families

HOLLY TOENSING

My eldest brother, Tom, took his own life in 1986, twenty years ago this past January. He was thirty-one years old. That this happened to our large, "perfect" family deepened the personal estrangement that ensued. That this happened while he was in seminary exacerbated the theological problems concerning his death that would haunt me for years. I wrote poems, essays, and letters that cathartically created my journey in and through grief. However, only within the past three years has a series of major convergences occurred that consistently compels me to re-examine this grief, push past my fears of speaking and writing about this publicly, and begin to open myself up to the mystery of whatever is to happen next.

But—I am nervous. So be patient with me if my voice is sometimes shaky or if I read my manuscript too much at times. I would never have guessed five years ago that I would be teaching at a church-affiliated university, that I would be attending church again and be very close to calling anyone from either of these two realms "family." The familiarity of your faces—like the faces of my blood family—has the capacity both to ground me and to leave me flailing about. My brother's suicide emotionally scattered and scarred my family forever. I sought consolation about his death in different kinds of Christian churches over the years but regularly felt the welcoming hand withdraw—silence and avoidance restricting my desperately-trying-to-beat-again heart. The "contamination" and the condemnation of this kind of death became painfully clear to me, and eventually, I just stopped talking about it, and I just stopped going to church. So, like a cat that thinks she is as thin as a flat sheet of paper lying on the ground she's hiding behind,—even though you and I can see her full-bodiedness plainly—I came to Knox with my soul flattened against my spine, though you have seen me in your midst for almost three years now. If I am ever going to be able to say that Knox is family to me, if I am ever going to be able to stop marking visitor in the fellowship pad and let my soul fill out into my body completely, I need Knox to know the story of my dealing with my brother's suicide.

83

Before I begin, I want to make clear that I do not speak for my family; I do not speak for all who have survived the suicide death of a loved one. Each of our stories, though they may be similar at times, are as distinctive as each individual who tells them. If given the opportunity to hear *another's* story of suicide, listen carefully for the human being *behind* it. That person is giving you a gift, not a formula. Similarly, I do not have *the* answer. In fact, I hope to convey to you how suicide deaths are distinctive, if not unique, in how questions linger, how ambiguity festers, and how paradox abounds. These are things that we, as survivors of deaths by suicide, must come to live with, even as much as they haunt us.

"A clean heart create for me, O God, and a steadfast spirit renew within me."[11]

> They reclined at table, and in the course of the meal Jesus said, "I give you my word, one of you is about to betray me, yes, one who is eating with me." They began to say to him, sorrowfully, one by one, "Surely, not I!"[12]

Tom did not leave a suicide note. Contrary to what everyone tends to think, most people who take their own lives do not leave notes, and even when they do, their notes are often unintelligible. Certainly, the notes left that *are* intelligible can be scathing if they name the person or the people who, from the perspective of the one who took her/his own life, drove the person to the horrid impasse. In this way, we survivors of my brother's death were blessed with his silence.

And yet, this blessing had its own curse, for the silence of a moment gave way to a chasm of years of *not knowing*. During the funeral week especially, I was simultaneously drawn to and distanced myself from my family, drawn to them because of our common blood and common shocking experience, distanced myself from them because of common doubt. *Surely, not I*, the text from the gospel says. Even though I can only speak for myself, I suspect that all my family members silently asked something similar of themselves and of one another: Surely, I did not drive my brother to do this, did I? Surely, my mom did not drive my brother to do this, did she—dad, Fumiko, Ellie, Nancy, Sandy, Scott.

I learned in graduate school that the way that question is asked classifies it as a rhetorical question—and the gospels are full of them. The

11. Ps 51:12
12. Mark 14:18–19

question expects a specific, particular answer that is already hinted at in the question itself. In this case, when the disciples ask, *surely, not I,* they boldly expect Jesus to answer, *oh no! I didn't mean you,* to calm the doubt that really lies behind the question. Jesus never gave that reassuring answer. Guilt and doubt seep into the souls of the survivors of suicide deaths in ways incomparable to other kinds of deaths.

As weeks, months, and years passed, a multitude of voices expressed *what possibly happened* to cause my brother's death. The voices swirled, collided, and echoed along the walls of this mystery: Maybe it was simply a chemical imbalance. He *had* placed himself on a strict diet to lose weight, *had* begun a rigorous exercise program, and *had* quit smoking *cold turkey.* Perhaps he had bipolar disease that had not been diagnosed during all of the psychological testing he had to undergo before entering seminary. A long-time family friend asked me once, confidentially, *was he gay and had married Fumiko only to try fit into what society expects?* Another suggested that, since he was in his second year of seminary, maybe he had he begun to see the *underside* of the Church and had become disenchanted. The question maddeningly remained the same over the years. The possible answers multiplied seemingly exponentially. In time, each of us had to develop a story to fill in the gaping hole like wood glue to make broken pieces strong enough to bear weight again.

"A clean heart create for me, O God, and a steadfast spirit renew within me."[13]

> [Judas said,] "I did wrong to deliver up an innocent man!" They [the chief priests and elders] retorted, "What is that to us? It is your affair!" So Judas flung the money into the temple and left. He went off and hanged himself.[14]

> The Son of Man is going the way the Scripture tells of him. Still, accursed be that man by whom the Son of Man is betrayed. It were better for him had he never been born.[15]

One way that I filled in part of the story of Tom's death had to do with the method by which he took his own life. He hung himself in a tree in a remote section of a state park outside St. Louis, Missouri. When I heard this, I immediately thought that Tom had chosen this method carefully,

13. Ps 51:12
14. Matt 27:4–5
15. Mark 14:21

intentionally drawing connections to Judas's death by hanging. In that first month after Tom died, I even remember dreaming him in a whole series of different scenarios of suicide that he *could have* chosen to use—gun, carbon monoxide, sleeping pills, etc. But I always pulled up short—not letting any of these scenarios play themselves out, none of them feeling like the way he would have chosen. None of them have the theological weight that hanging does, and Tom was, after all, in seminary.

Suicide is the response that Judas takes when he acknowledges the depth of his betrayal of Jesus, as Matthew's text conveys. Did Tom feel like he had betrayed Jesus or God in some way? Tom strongly felt *called* into the ministry—even before seminary, he had been a missionary in Japan for three years. Had he later felt the hand of God retreat in some way, leaving him spiritually isolated? Were Jesus' words regarding Judas, *better never to have been born*, echoing in his head as he jumped from his car's rooftop—or *cursed is the one who hangs from a tree?*

Influenced by a Christian heritage that includes a divine command not to kill/murder, our cultural language *criminalizes* suicide; one *commits* suicide just as one might commit a murder or a rape. Our society desires to bring criminals to justice by prosecuting them in law courts for the sake of the victims of the crimes. In the case of suicides, however, this desire is frustrated since the "murderer" and the "victim" are one and the same person.

This results in an excess of ambiguity that Christianity attempted—and still attempts—to resolve by creating a particular concept of the afterlife for suicides that stresses punishment. Taking its cue, I think, from the Judas story, by believing that suicide represents the epitome of separation from God, Christianity historically claimed that the person who takes her or his own life may have avoided human punishment for the crime but will not avoid God's punishment, certain condemnation in eternal hell. In the twenty years of dealing with my brother's suicide, *no more than three or four months ever pass by before I hear this condemnation in one form or another.* As you can imagine, that makes an impression on a person. The taboo of talking about it only reinforces that condemnation.

The theology of punishment for suicides has been—and in some cases continues to be—embodied in Church practices, such as not allowing the bodies of those who took their own lives to be brought onto church premises or buried in Christian cemeteries. A few days before my brother's funeral, I asked one of my sisters why we weren't having Tom's body in the church. She answered, *I don't know*, in a mildly severe, hushed tone, which cued me not to pursue the question any further. As the years passed, I became more and more angry at the church of my upbringing for this apparent rejection. However, I found out from a former pastor a little more than a year ago that my *parents* had made the decision about Tom's body, not the church: The Missouri Synod Lutheran Church by that time *did* allow suicide bodies to be brought into their churches. A similar story was conveyed to me in the spring of 2003 by one of my graduate students at Xavier. He told me that just the semester before, in the fall of 200, a Christian cemetery in the Cincinnati area agreed to bury his brother, but when the family brought the remains after the funeral, they were initially denied because cemetery personnel had, in the meantime, found out that the cause of death was suicide.

The concept of punishment for suicide permeates our cultural language, too. While it omits direct reference to God, the popular 1998 Robin Williams film, "What Dreams May Come," horrifyingly depicts a descent to hell and then, if that weren't bad enough, to hell's farthest reaches for those who have committed suicide. The pain they had when they were living becomes, in the afterlife, their perpetual, irredeemable psychological torment, their own "hell."

As contentious as Tom's and my relationship often was before his death and as angry as I often was with him for how he cut off all relationship with us in his death, I never wished physical or psychological hell upon him. That seemed—that seems like such a cruel response.

And yet, the well-intentioned comments about heaven, such as, *he's in a better place now*, or *he's no longer in pain*, equally dismayed me because, to those of us living with what felt like unbearable pain, those comments cruelly seemed to tempt us with a *way out*.

"A clean heart create for me, O God, and a steadfast spirit renew within me."[16]

> When she [A servant-girl of the high priest] noticed Peter warming himself, she looked at him more closely and said, "You too were with Jesus of Nazareth." But he denied it: "I do not know what you are talking about! What are you getting at?" The servant girl, keeping an eye on him, started again to tell the bystanders, "This man is one of them." Once again he denied it. A little later, the bystanders said to Peter once more, "You are certainly one of

16. Ps 51:12

them! You are a Galilean, are you not?" He began to curse, and to swear, "I do not even know the man you are talking about!"[17]

" . . . You should issue an order having the tomb kept under surveillance until the third day. Otherwise, his disciples may go and steal him and tell the people, 'He has been raised from the dead!' This final imposture would be worse than the first." Pilate told them, "You have a guard. Go and secure the tomb as best you can." So they went and kept it under surveillance of the guard, after fixing a seal to the stone.[18]

I didn't want to place Tom in hell, but neither did I want to place him in heaven. I didn't know *what to do* with him, what kind of afterlife to imagine for him. This is, I believe, beginning to reflect many people's attitudes. Though there seems to be a *slow* movement away from the punishment concept, people are hesitant to assure heaven for suicides. In recent years, when I have expressed the thought to others that I might try to come up with a new theology of suicide, I have heard several times, *but you aren't going to say anything positive about suicide, are you?* So I have felt pressure to keep Tom "hanging" or to keep him in a box.

By encapsulating Tom's suicide, I adamantly claimed that he and he alone did this. His wife, Fumiko, had nothing to do with it. My family had nothing to do with it. I didn't have anything to do with it. God/Jesus didn't have anything to do with it. He did this on his own. By isolating him/his action completely, I insulated myself from any hint of possibility that aspects of his environment—no matter how general or specific—influenced or contributed to how he felt and responded to things. This way, I could deny that his death touched me. I could pronounce him excommunicated just as loudly as his death pronounced the same on our family.

But in separating Tom from everything, have I negated the very thing I thought I was protecting? I thought I could keep God if I denied Tom, protecting God from Tom's rejection, or was it, I could keep Tom if I denied God, protecting Tom from God's rejection—or still yet, keep myself if I denied them both and stopped feeling about either of them?

I no longer want to deny Tom, God, or myself. I want to be relieved of my centurion duties. I am tired of standing guard at negation.

17. Mark 14:67–71
18. Matt 27:64–66

"A clean heart create for me, O God, and a steadfast spirit renew within me."[19]

> Meanwhile, Mary stood weeping beside the tomb. Even as she wept, she stopped to peer inside, and there she saw two angels in dazzling robes. One was seated at the head and the other at the foot of the place where Jesus' body had lain. "Woman," they asked her, "why are you weeping?" She answered them, "Because the Lord has been taken away, and I do not know where they have put him." She had no sooner said this than she turned around and caught sight of Jesus standing there. But she did not know him. "Woman," he asked her, "why are you weeping? Who is it you are looking for?" She supposed he was the gardener, so she said, "Sir, if you are the one who carried him off, tell me where you have laid him, and I will take him away." Jesus then said, "Mary! . . . Do not cling to me."[20]

About two-and-a-half years ago, a new, dear friend of mine who had heard significant pieces of my story regarding my brother's death looked me in the eye and said, *you keep talking about hanging, your brother hanging himself, the hanging relationships afterward. I think you're the one hanging!* A few minutes later, she said, *what if, just what if, the box where you feel you have had to place Tom is empty?*

Inwardly, I reeled in disbelief and anger. *How dare she make such claims! Me the one hanging? Empty*?! I began, *you mean to tell me,* but as the words came tumbling out of my mouth intending to express my incredulity, they instead started to paint pictures of Jesus' passion story in my head and began to transform my soul, *you mean to tell me, that for nearly twenty years, I've been standing guard at a tomb that might be empty?!* In that moment, the futility of my attempts to protect gave way, and I began laughing at the absurdity of the possible scene.

For the first time, I felt like I could take steps away from "the tomb," turn around, and actually look at it, look into it as Mary did. I felt like someone had said to me, *you don't have to do this anymore.* I was finally released from guard duty, and I, in turn, could release Tom and God—if I ever had them! Two weeks later when I was in Minnesota, I went to Tom's gravesite for the first time ever by myself and willingly since Tom died. I hauled out a lawn chair and sat for the better part of an hour or two looking at the grave, mostly just pondering what it meant to think of it being empty but also,

19. Ps 51:12
20. John 20:11, 14–17

sometimes, reading Tom's and my favorite poetry aloud—into the grave, into the sky, into the trees, into my body, anywhere my voice would reach.

I still don't know where, exactly, Tom *is*, and I still cringe and rage and weep when I hear echoes of punishment in hell for suicides. But I'm not sure I understand anymore the dilemma of "not hell, but not heaven either" that I felt I knew so well for such a long time. If I linger now at the tomb, it is not because I am clinging to Tom; I may be trying to keep anyone from putting him back inside.

"A clean heart create for me, O God, and a steadfast spirit renew within me."[21]

> Then he addressed this parable to them: "Who among you, if he has a hundred sheep, and loses one of them, does not leave the ninety-nine in the wasteland and follow the lost one until he finds it. And when he finds it, he puts it on his shoulders in jubilation. Once arrived home, he invites friends and neighbors in and says to them, 'Rejoice with me because I have found my lost sheep.' . . . What woman, if she has ten pieces of silver and loses one, does not light a lamp and sweep the house in a diligent search until she has retrieved what she has lost? And when she finds it, she calls in her friends and neighbors to say, 'Rejoice with me! I have found the silver piece that I lost.'"[22]

Last summer, I participated in a week-long Jesuit retreat. I used it to continue to work on some of the remaining theological questions I have about my brother's suicide. A particularly poignant day for me began when we were asked us to ponder the *lost and found* parables of Luke chapter 15. I began the day's meditation by reading and re-reading those parables, at first feeling no particular connection to them. I am fortunate to have enough money that if I drop a coin or two, I don't necessarily go searching high and low for them, and the last time I was around sheep was back in high school when one of my best friends and her family kept and showed them; I don't remember her telling me about any lost sheep and having to go find them hither and yonder.

But then, when I focused on the part of the story that mentioned the persistence of the searcher, I recalled full force bits and pieces of what I had been told during the funeral week of my brother's suicide. My parents got the call from Fumiko on Monday night. Tom had not come home Sunday night after he said that he was going to the seminary's library. Right away, Dad tried

21. Ps 51:12

22. Luke 15:3–9

to get a flight to St. Louis but couldn't get one until the first thing Tuesday morning. When he arrived, he helped Fumiko think through all the possible places where Tom might be—any favorite places of theirs, restaurants, movie theatres, city parks—they checked all these. Dad went to the seminary and asked his current classmates if they had seen him. He asked his professors. He urgently asked seminary administrators. With a picture of Tom in his hand, he stopped anyone he could on the campus and asked if Tom had been seen. He sought out the St. Louis police and asked to fill out a missing persons report, but the police told him that such reports are really only for children, that adults who go missing, well, they're *missing* for a reason and don't want to be found. Shamelessly, my Dad went to all the local TV and radio stations to beg them to let him on the air to plead with Tom to come home, if he were listening, and to ask people to keep an eye out for him. For four days, my Dad tirelessly searched for my brother. Unfortunately, the story didn't end as well as the stories in Luke/ My Dad was not able to find Tom alive and, rejoicing, carry him home on his shoulders for a homecoming party. Our gathering was much more somber and shocking. *And yet,* I thought, *if my Dad could be that persistent in trying to find Tom, how much more so could God be?* I've begun to think that maybe God found Tom first.

"A clean heart create for me, O God, and a steadfast spirit renew within me."[23]

> During the meal he [Jesus] took bread, blessed and broke it, and gave it to them. "Take this," he said, "this is my body." He likewise took a cup, gave thanks and passed it to them: "This is my blood, the blood of the covenant, to be poured out on behalf of many."[24]

Perhaps I was still unsteady on my feet after having stood guard for so long. Maybe I leaned too far into the tomb to try to examine *thoroughly* just how empty the tomb *really* was, but the fact is that I, myself, fell into the tomb.

A virus attacked my thyroid almost three years ago, making me excessively hyper twenty-four hours a day for two months, then swinging me the other direction, making me hypo for another two months—with very little that could be done medically because it was a virus. My body and my mind were utterly exhausted by the fall of 2003. The months of that fall passed with increased difficulty, and, eventually, I realized to my horror that I was suicidal. In the care of a mental health professional, I spent about

23. Ps 51:12
24. Mark 14:22–24

four months clawing my way out of that tomb, oftentimes having to repeat to myself, *I am not like my brother Tom; I am not my brother.*

A year ago last December, just months into a year-long pact with myself that I would at least *try* life again, that I would at least *practice* being alive each day, I came to the Longest Night Service here at Knox with remnants of death clinging to me. When I saw that the communion table had been set up, I almost just kept walking, just passing through the church. Ever since my brother's suicide, I have felt uncomfortable with Communion, in part, I believe, because the condemnation theology of suicide pushed me to believe that Tom and others like him did not figure into "the many" for whom Christ's death was effective; thus, in taking Communion, I somehow felt complicit in that condemnation. But I forced myself to stay that for the service, telling myself I didn't *have* to participate if I didn't want to. Being there, *trying,* was enough.

The service was meaningful in many ways, making possible my decision to come forward to receive communion. My turn came, and, with no irony lost on me, I found it unsettling to be standing before Tom [York]—the pastor my brother never became. He called me by name, *Holly,* then said, *the Bread of Life given for you.* There was no mistake. There were no other Hollys in line, and he was looking at me and holding the bread out to me. It is difficult to describe the juxtaposition of my emotions in those brief seconds, even though, for me, time seemed to warp into slow motion. Internally, I was yelling at him, *Oh yeah?! You're offering me life? You better not be offering me something you'll only regret later or have to retract later once you find out I've been thinking this entire time about my brother's suicide and my own near brush with suicide—the epitome of separation from God. Are you sure you really can offer me life?* And yet, simultaneously, all the years of cultural and religious shame about suicide that had been pushed my way, that clung to me like iron shavings to a magnet, scattered as if the polarity had suddenly shifted, and I wanted to hear those words of life again and again and again, a balm to soothe where death had been. If I released my brother, Tom, and God when I stepped off my guard duty the year before, they *together* entered me in the breaking of bread during that Longest Night Service, bringing hope to me once again that church *can* be a place of healing and can be a place of *practicing life,* not death—for all of us—in all the ways we break bread together.

∾

Resources in Islam for Solace and Healing
*For Family and Friends of a Loved One Who has
Died by Suicide*

JAMAL RAHMAN

On almost any issue of ethics, and certainly on the question of suicide, Muslims lean heavily on the Quran as their primary resource for wisdom and guidance. The holy book is a collection of divine revelations transmitted mysteriously to the Prophet Muhammad through angel Gabriel over a twenty-three-year period during the seventh century.

To supplement insight from the Quran, Muslims also consult three other resources. The first is the collected sayings (*hadith*) and behavior (*sunnah*) of the Prophet. The second is the wisdom of jurists and spiritual teachers. Because Islam has no official priesthood or religious ordination, the opinions of legal scholars and spiritual insights of Islamic sages carry special weight. The third resource is *ijtihad*, which means individual reasoning. When, after consulting the Quran, the Prophet, and the scholars, one is still unclear about what to do, one is directed to use the inner resources of mind and heart to come to an understanding. Muhammad famously said, *even if the religious judge advises you about earthly matters, first consult your heart.*

Case Study

Several years ago, I was asked to counsel a South Asian Muslim family that was trying to cope with anxiety and pain because a young female relative of sixteen had died by hanging herself. They were receiving advice and counseling from professionals but were especially eager to receive guidance from Islamic sources.

We began our session with a period of meditative silence and Quranic recitations, and then the family asked a number of anxious questions about suicide and the fate of the beloved relative in the afterworld. *What is the exact verse in the Quran that pertains to suicide?* I mentioned the verse in chapter 4, "You shall not kill yourselves. God is Merciful towards you.

Anyone who commits these transgressions, maliciously and deliberately, we will condemn him to Hell."[25] I asked them to take note of the words *malicious* and *deliberate* and explained that the young person's action was neither malicious nor deliberate. The deep anguish of her pain over a prolonged period of time had clouded her mind and clenched her heart. She was not able to think clearly, and her feelings were numbed. No matter what people in the community might say, I asked them to remember that God is a witness to the truth. I then recited the Quranic verse, "Is it not enough that your Sustainer is a witness?"[26]

There were some nervous questions about hell. What was my personal view about hell? I offered my view that, for me and the majority of Muslims, the vivid descriptions of heaven and hell are metaphorical, meant to incline the heart of the person to do righteous deeds and avoid malicious transgressions. Then, because it seemed important to buttress this personal opinion with something from the four resources mentioned in the introduction, I related the well-known story of the Prophet, who was so deeply moved by the sight of a mother tenderly caring for her little child that he remarked to his companions, *look at this woman and her concern for her child. Would she hurl her own child into a blazing fire with her own hands? I tell you, God loves us much more than this mother loves her child.*

I also told the story of the beloved ninth-century century saint Rabia, who was seen rushing through the town with a torch in one hand and a pail of water in the other. Her mission, she said, was to torch the splendors of heaven and quench the fires of hell so that when we worship God, we do it not out of fear of hell or desire for heaven but for the sake of God's everlasting beauty.

The discussion turned to God and forgiveness. What if the young woman had committed a great wrong in the eyes of God? *To God we belong, and to God we are returning*, says the Quran. Did she not rebel against Divine Will by taking her own life? Will God readily forgive? On the same subject of forgiveness, one of the relatives cried out that she felt deeply ashamed for having been so unmindful of the girl's anguish. Would God ever forgive her for being so insensitive?

I sought to reassure them that, in every case, God forgives. I recited the following verse, "O my servants, who have transgressed against your own soul. Despair not of the Mercy of God, for God forgives all sins, for God is

25. Quran 4:29
26. Quran 41:53

oft-forgiving and most Merciful."[27] I reminded them of the Quranic insight that God, the Absolute Mystery, is incomprehensible to human faculties but is perceivable through divine attributes, of which ninety-nine are mentioned in the holy book. Of all the attributes, compassion is repeated most often. The essence of Divinity in the Quran is Compassion. All but one of the one hundred fourteen chapters of the Quran begin with the phrase, *in the name of God, Boundlessly Merciful and Compassionate.* God is capable of wrath, but in a *hadith*, God tells Muhammad, *My mercy overspreads my wrath*, and in the Quran, God says, "My mercy overspreads everything."[28]

A couple of people lamented that when they consulted several imams about the suicide, the advice they received was contradictory, and some of it was distressing. How were they to know, they politely asked, that my advice was authentic? Again, I reminded them that there is no official priesthood in Islam. The title is self-appointed or bestowed by a specific neighborhood or community. Knowledge varies from one imam to another, and my knowledge also might be faulty. That is why Islam encourages every Muslim to take responsibility for developing his or her own knowledge. It is noteworthy that the second-most used word in the Quran after Allah is *ilm*, meaning knowledge, and what is most valued is heart knowledge. The Prophet said, *every Muslim is his own priest*, and advised us to, *move from knowledge of the tongue to knowledge of heart.* The Quran tells us to plead, *O God, expand me in knowledge.* Daily, the Prophet Muhammad cried out, *O God, may I see things as they really are.* On such a complex and sensitive matter as suicide, a dry, theoretical pronouncement of theology is a poor substitute for a heart-felt experiential understanding of the issue.

One of the imams had advised them not to cry because the tears might be an obstacle for the soul of the deceased on its journey in those mysterious realms. Is this advice rooted in the Quran, they wanted to know. My understanding, I told them, is just the opposite. The Quran says, "It is God who grants you laughter and tears."[29] To most spiritual teachers, this means that tears are sacred. *Your tears are holy*, I told them, and I recited the holy utterance of the thirteenth-century sage Rumi, *weep like the waterwheel, so that sweet herbs may grow in the courtyard of your soul.*

I moved from discussion of tears to that of feelings. All feelings are sacred. Again, this understanding is grounded in the Quran: "It is God who

27. Quran 39:53
28. Quran 7:156
29. Quran 53:43

has given you sight, hearing and feelings."[30] Feelings are a gift from God, and we are asked to honor them. Feelings that are considered negative, such as guilt and shame, are simply energies that beg our attention. They have an edge only because they are separated from us. When we allow ourselves, little by little and with compassion for self, to acknowledge, enfold, and integrate these feelings, the negative feelings are healed and transformed into life-affirming energies. Something shifts in us. We become more complete as a human being. We move closer to God. I introduced a spiritual practice called *sacred holding* that heals and integrates difficult feelings.

What other Islamic advice did I have for them? I requested them to gather regularly in community to talk about their feelings and pray together. About the need for community, the Quran says, "Truly, by token of time, human beings are in loss except those who have faith and do righteous deeds and gather together in teaching of truth and patient perseverance."[31] I told them that by doing the five-times-a-day prayer together whenever possible, they would become more conscious of God. The admonition to *be conscious of God* is the most often repeated advice in the Quran. "For the one who remains conscious of God," says the Quran, "God provides a way of emergence in ways one could never imagine,"[32] and, "Truly in the remembrance of God do hearts find rest."[33] I also mentioned a *hadith* that says, in effect, that God remembers us even better when we remember God in the context of community.

I repeated the timeless advice of spiritual teachers, that in times of difficulty, the most effective healing comes from feeling close to God. The Quran advises us to persist in the work of becoming conscious of God no matter how difficult the work, "After the difficulty is the easing; after the difficulty is the easing. So, when you are finished, strive again and in your Lord aspire."[34] Eventually, healing and ease of heart will happen because, as a *hadith* says, *the heart of the believer is between two fingers of the Merciful, Who turns it wherever He desires.*

Besides ritual body prayer in community, they asked, could I suggest another technique to sustain closeness to God? I shared my favorite practice, called "Adoring Divine Heart." The Quran says that God is both outside

30. Quran 23:78, 32:9
31. Quran 103:1–3
32. Quran 65:2–3
33. Quran 13:28
34. Quran 94:5–8

of us (*zahir*) and within us (*batin*), specifically in the human heart. In an exquisite revelation called *hadith qudsi*, God said, *I cannot be contained in the space of the earth, I cannot be contained in the space of the heavens, but I can be contained in the space of the pure loving heart.* Divine Heart is in human heart! "Adoring Divine Heart" involves focusing on one's heart and with deep sincerity and feeling, telling the heart repeatedly, *I love you* or *Thank you, God.* This expression of love and gratitude opens a passageway between human heart and Divine Heart. One becomes illumined with what sages call *Glow of Presence.*

I ended the session by saying that the All-Merciful God joyously enfolds each and every retuning soul with tenderness and compassion. No matter what the circumstances of the return to God, the journey in God in those mysterious realms is unspeakably beautiful. The Quran says, "O serene soul, return to your Sustainer pleased and pleasing in His sight. Join my righteous servants and enter my Paradise."[35]—or in the words of Rumi, *a lovesick nightingale among owls, you caught the scent of roses and flew to the rose garden.*

The Ancient Technique of Sacred Holding

This powerful technique can be used when difficult feelings come up in us. Take time to follow these steps at the earliest opportunity.

- The first step is to allow yourself to experience. Tell yourself that every feeling is valid. Ask yourself, *what feeling is coming up in me?* Name that feeling. Maybe it is anger, sadness, jealousy, or bitterness.

- In the second step, ask yourself, *where do I hold this feeling in my body?* Locate the feeling. It definitely has a resting place in your body. We are able to experience a feeling because it registers as a physical sensation somewhere in the body.

- In the third and very important step, receive this "holding" in your body with compassion for yourself. Encompass the physical sensations in your body with the embrace of your soul. From your heart, send love and mercy to this physical holding. Talk tenderly to yourself; cultivate a gentle rapport with yourself. Tell yourself, for example, *I'm sorry you feel this. This is difficult. Let me tenderly support you.* At

---

35. Quran 89:27–28

this time, there is no need to fix or analyze the sensations, simply a need to be present with the holding for as long as you want. This is the process of trembling.

- In the fourth step, focus gently on the holding in your body and intend to inhale and exhale through that part of you. Allow divine breath to caress you there.

These four steps acknowledge, nurture, and integrate those feelings in God's Light. Slowly, as you persist with this technique, an amazing shift occurs; that which was negative, irksome, and painful integrates and now transforms into a source of strength and wholeness in you.

Bibliography

Rahman, Jamal. *The Fragrance of Faith: The Enlightened Heart of Islam*. Bath, England: Book Foundation, 2004., 109–110.

"Somewhere Over the Rainbow"

REVEREND DONALD M. MACKENZIE

As for artists and poets, an "openness to the new" needs to be an important component in any pastoral sensibility. I am writing this essay with the hope that it will be an encouragement to pastors and religious leaders, providing comfort and guidance at a time of suicide.

As a pastor, I have had many occasions to be with and provide counsel to people who have contemplated suicide or have attempted suicide and failed. With each of these encounters, I have been deeply moved by coming face to face with the total loss of hope and how easily that can come when one is simply too tired to move ahead, too tired to try to imagine what hope might look like, too tired to know how it might feel. The line between having hope and not having it is so thin, it is frightening.

Some time ago, a family approached me with the news that the daughter in the family had died by suicide. She had been an office worker in another city and had also been a singer in nightclubs in that city. The family came to me and to our church (they were not members) because they understood that we would honor the reality of a suicide and be willing to name the truth of it during worship, during the memorial service. It was a relief for me to know they wished to name the reality of suicide. The shame that suicide evokes now in our culture can make it very difficult for families to be willing to take this necessary step toward healing, especially in the midst of such deep grief, along with the internal recognition that we all carry of that thin line between hope and hopelessness.

As we were planning the memorial service, the father mentioned that his daughter's favorite song was "Somewhere Over the Rainbow." She loved to sing it and to listen to it. He asked if it could be included in the service. As it happened, I like the song, too, but my first reaction was that it was not appropriate for worship. Providentially, I didn't say that because, as I thought about it, I realized that the song is about hope, and not just any hope but a deep sense of hope for a kind of healing. Dorothy wants to get home. The Scarecrow wants brains. The Tin Woodman wants a heart. The Cowardly Lion wants courage. Their shared need of that one thing that would make them complete brings them together on their journey toward the Emerald City. The miracle of the story is that, in the end, they each discover that they have had everything they needed all along. That is a very strong and important theological statement. We each carry a sense of being incomplete, and yet, from a theological point of view, we do have everything we need. Our persistent estrangement from that is a strong part of what it means to be human.

At the memorial service, during the Statement of Remembrance and Hope, I played a recording of Judy Garland singing "Somewhere Over the Rainbow" and reflected on what I have said above. As I was preparing for this, I realized that for the family of the one who had died, the thing that would put each of them on the yellow brick road to the Emerald City would have been the hope for a chance to connect materially with the daughter who loved that song, the daughter who lost hope. So now, where would her family find hope?

I used a couple of lines from Emily Dickinson's poem "Hope." The poem evokes a sense of being able to be lifted, a sense of how singing is, in itself, an act of hope, and finally, a sense of steadfastness. Again, the theology, the question of the role and place of God in that moment, came through in the poem. In fact, I would say that one could substitute the word "God" for the word "hope" and not change the meaning at all.

That led me to Romans 5:3-5, "We know that affliction makes for endurance, and endurance for tested virtue, and tested virtue for hope. And this hope will not leave us disappointed, because the love of God has been poured in our hearts through the Holy Spirit who has been given to us." Hope does not disappoint us. God does not disappoint us.

The experience of the suicide of someone we love brings feelings of loss and anger, along with the sense that we might have been able to do something to prevent the death. The grief and anguish that accompany those feelings, finally, cannot be described in words. We want desperately to find that we are actually back in Kansas and that everything is all right. When someone has died, we are not all right. Things have changed. And yet, as the Archbishop of Canterbury, William Temple, said in the first part of the twentieth century, *tragedy is the experience of irreparable brokenness. In God's eyes, nothing is ever irreparably broken.* We do get home, and we have all the brains, all the heart, and all the courage that we need because God's love has been poured into us through the Holy Spirit that has been given to us. Even though one person has lost hope, we have been given the possibility to recover it and move ahead.

Had I not been forced to look *outside the box*, I might have missed a wonderful opportunity to connect faith to this song, a song about hope in a film about hope. They came to my church looking for hope and reassurance and gave me the key to unlock it for them.

Notes in Response to a Suicide for a Clergy Person

Rabbi Ted Falcon, Ph.D.

The second funeral of my career as a rabbi was for a wife and mother who was forty-one years old. It was in August of my first job as assistant rabbi at a progressive Reform synagogue in West Los Angeles. In June, we had driven across country from Cincinnati, Ohio, where I was ordained a rabbi after a five-and-a-half-year graduate program at the Hebrew Union College—Jewish Institute of Religion. No one during that time had talked about dealing with suicide, except perhaps in theory. The father and three children who walked into my office that afternoon were not theoretical, and they hardly sought a theoretical response from me.

As the assistant rabbi, I received requests from the general community. The senior rabbi, who had been there almost twenty-five years, was the one the congregants went to, which was proper, of course, since I was only the second assistant ever to serve that community. When calls came in from the nearby ICU at the UCLA Hospital in Westwood Village, they were directed to me. I still remember standing at the bedside of an older man suffering from a serious heart attack. He looked me over—all twenty-six years of me—and shook his head. *You're not a real rabbi,* he announced. *Send me a real rabbi!* Looking back, I appreciate his perceptions. I'm sure I looked far more like a student than one who could legitimately perform the functions of a rabbi.

The four members of the family entered my office. I pulled in an extra two chairs. The kids were twelve, nine, and seven, a boy, a girl, and another boy. After sitting down, the father pulled a sheet of paper from his pocket, unfolded it, and handed it to me. It was a photocopy of a handwritten letter. As I read it, I tried to look calmer than I felt. Their wife and mother had been thinking about it for a long time. This was no sudden act of a moment. Her note very directly related her intentions, rooted in her pain. She wanted them to know that it was not their fault. She was sorry. She had reached the end of her pain.

I have no idea what our conversation consisted of that afternoon. I recall receiving additional information. She had driven her car into a lonely canyon, pulled off the road, and taken pills she had been saving for some time. When she hadn't returned that evening, the police were called. They found her a few days later. The note was on the seat next to her body.

After helping make the arrangements the father/husband wished for the funeral, I scheduled a meeting with them at their home for the following day. When they left, I went into the senior rabbi's office to seek his counsel.

"What do I do?" I asked.

"I don't know," he said. "I don't know. But tell me what you do."

My assumption was that working as an assistant rabbi would allow me to be with an experienced rabbi who could provide aspects of my education that were missing from rabbinical school. My senior rabbi was either honest enough to admit his own lack of experience, or he was telling me that I needed to respond in my own way. At that moment, I felt abandoned. I imagined that was a very distant reflection of what that family was experiencing.

The next day, I met them in their home. The woman was an artist, and their home was in the hills, and it was lovely. There was every indication that the family living there was happy. Her art studio was even more surprising. Her favorite motif appeared to be the sun, and in paintings and ceramics, her bright and lively suns lit up her workspace.

She had not been an overtly unhappy woman, though I learned that she had gone through bouts of depression. She seemed productive as an artist and available as a wife and mother. Yet, she had taken her own life, and she had planned it well. What was I to make of such a reality? It's one thing to talk about suicide as an abstract reality; it's quite another to encounter it in the beautiful hills of Bel Air. And what kind of response could I make that might be helpful for this family?

Traditionally, of course, Jewish teachings deny a full funeral to one who dies by their own hand. There is to be no eulogy. But that restriction was quickly dismissed by the ancient rabbis, who decided that no one in their right mind kills themselves. Therefore, the death reflects mental instability or illness, and so that person and their family deserve the benefit of full mourning rituals.

But with suicide, there is an additional layer of guilt carried by the family: In what ways are we responsible for this tragedy? Were there things we could have done? How are we to live with the terrible weight of this death-by-choice?

I remember doing my best to talk openly about such matters. Because the family had no connection to my congregation, we dropped into each other's lives for the event of the funeral and the beginning of the period of grieving. They were not observant, so the traditional frame of Jewish mourning could offer them little comfort. I would like to think that our conversations were of some solace, but I realized later how naive I was at that time to the depths of their pain.

What struck me was the brightness of her artwork. My experience was that art often offered the artist an outlet not only for the brightness of life but also for the darkness. The shadow side of one's identity can often be dealt with more directly through artistic expression. Here was a woman who was not able to confront her demons either directly or symbolically. There was really no way for us to know what shadows she carried; we had evidence that she could only release the pressure that had built up within her through ending her life.

After the funeral, her best friend, another artist, gifted me with an etching that I still have forty years later. Her friend was a bundle of light, yet her etching aches with darkness. The couple depicted in the etching personified the shadow. It's not a particularly pleasant piece of art, but I keep it to help me remember the possible consequences of the inability to honor the darkness we all carry. We maintain balance in our lives only when we are able to honor both sides of our beings.

Many years have passed since then. Over time, I have experienced many more deaths but, thankfully, no other successful suicide attempts. I have learned that each death is unique, just as each life has its own integrity. I had once asked my senior rabbi for the way I should conduct the funeral service for the woman who had killed herself. I imagined that there was *the* way.

There is no *the* way. Each unique moment bears its own invitation, and we are most able to support each other when we hear the call and respond with being as present as possible. Because I went on to study for a doctorate at the California School for Professional Psychology, I have had the opportunity to sit with those who were actively contemplating suicide, and I know that there is no single answer that can speak to the pain such persons carry.

There have been times when such meetings have allowed me to find the deeply despairing places in my own being and to understand from the inside something of the intensity of aloneness and anguish another might be experiencing. I have learned that the willingness to enter openly into the valley of such shadow is often the beginning of the healing that might be. I have also learned that we cannot control another's self-destructive behavior—at least not forever.

I remember a story that Martin Buber, one of the greatest Jewish philosophers of the twentieth century, related in one of his books. A student had come to him, he thought, for a brief consultation in his university office, but later, Buber learned that the young man had killed himself some time following that brief conversation. It was a turning point for Buber, who asked, *what does a person come to another for at an hour of great need? Only to hear, "nevertheless, there is meaning."*

Nevertheless, there is meaning.

Reflections on Suicide in a Clergy Family

Reverend Paul Tunkle

Susan was one of my parishioners. She worked for a counseling agency in our community. I was rector of the downtown Episcopal church. Lea died at age twenty-two from suicide on August 24, 1997. Susan went into work and mentioned to another counselor colleague that her rector's daughter had died by suicide. The woman was a member of a church in another Christian tradition.

When she heard Susan, she shook her head and responded, "Uhmm, uhmm, uhmm, Satan's gonna have his way with that church."

Thus began a journey of sorrow, loss, grief, anger, betrayal, and spiritual crisis.

Lea had made three attempts over an eighteen month period leading up to her death. The possibility of her death by suicide was ever present with us. Parents who have lost their children in this way can understand the feelings of deep anguish, loss of heart, and a sense of profound failure. If that were not enough to overload my emotional life, I was also forced to deal with the question of, *where was God?*

I had prayed for Lea's healing every day during the months before her death. I had prayed for her healing the morning after her death, prior to learning of the discovery of her body in the parking lot of an abandoned Sears. She had shot herself the night before, but for us, she was missing and not yet dead until we heard of the discovery. So, after all that prayer and faith in the future, Lea was dead. What did this mean for my faith and belief in a loving God? How could I cling to that belief in the face of so much evidence to the contrary? And how could I continue to preach God's love when I was so uncertain of its truth?

With so many questions and so much pain, I tried to soldier on as pastor of the church. I preached my questions and my doubts. The people of the church were loving and kind and patient. Three members of the congregation later told me that their decision to devote their lives to ordained ministry stemmed from that time of my asking such profound questions. But not all felt that way.

Two key elected leaders in the congregation came to see me within six weeks of Lea's death. They suggested I might need a lawyer because the church would be voting to ask for my resignation. My question was, *on what grounds?* Their words still sting. *Your daughter's death by suicide has invalidated your credentials to be our ordained leader.* I can think of no crueler words ever spoken to me in my life. In a moment, I faced not only Lea's death but loss of job and security, loss of house and home, and loss of vocation and ministry. It turned out that one of these leaders had a daughter at risk for suicide. The other had attempted, and his wife had intervened just before he pulled the trigger. I did not know that at the time, and I did not understand how deeply threatening and frightening suicide can be. For these two and others with them, every time they looked at me, they were reminded of their worst nightmare, and since they could not face their own, they sought to remove me in the hope that it would somehow help them.

There is an expression all too painfully true at times. *The church is the only institution that shoots its wounded.* Would this have happened if Lea had died of leukemia or from a car accident? I doubt it. I was indicted and convicted by some of being the bad parent who had allowed this to happen to his child. Being in their minds a felon, I could no longer present a wholesome example to the flock. I was sent reeling out of control and felt the spiral fall into blackness, but God is, indeed, kind and loving. God sent me other members of the parish who stood by me and lifted me up and resisted this movement to hurt me, and they prevailed. I carry the scars, but they remind me of the healers who sustained me and rescued me.

Within weeks of Lea's death, I was confronted with a parishioner whose death was by suicide. I was to speak at the graveside. Other ministers spoke at the funeral, and suicide was never mentioned. When my turn came, I went straight to the issue. As the body was being lowered into the grave, I asked people to throw in other things that needed burial that day. I asked them to bury any thought that they were somehow responsible for this death. I asked them to bury any notion that they could have saved him. I asked them to bury any belief that this death was a sin beyond God's forgiveness. And I asked them to bury any thought that he had been consigned to hell—later, when people asked me if I thought Lea was in hell, I would answer, *no, she is in heaven as someone who died of a terminal illness, but I am left here, and this is hell for me.* After the funeral, one by one, people gravitated to me and asked me how I knew to say those words, how I knew what was gnawing at their hearts and how I knew what they needed so that they could cope and heal. I began to see a new shape to ministry and a renewed sense of call from God.

Why can a pastor not be fully human? Why can those of us who follow a savior who was human in every way as we are not be accorded that same privilege of being human? Why can a minister not have tragedy and illness in their own family? Lea's death demanded of me a radical honesty before God and before people that would seek no compromise. She was forthright and resolute, and I would honor her in this way. I could not issue platitudes or say what I thought people wanted to hear. I had to acknowledge that what I knew of God was gone, and a new reality was emerging, the shape of which was entirely unclear to me. I have found that more people seek a space to ask questions than a place where answers are readily pronounced. I was a living question, and the answers may be a lifetime in coming. I accept this way of living as my commitment to the truth as I see it.

I found to my surprise that suicide is no stranger to the life of ordained leaders. When I asked a representative of the Church Insurance Company how common this was, they said, sadly, that it was something they dealt with often.

"You mean other ministers have lost children to suicide?"

"No, we mean many ministers themselves have died by suicide."

Once we take the courage to speak of these things, we discover that we are members of a community. To quote Sting in his song "Message in a Bottle," "seems I'm not alone in being alone."[36]

Healing from Lea's death was a long and intense journey. Many marriages do not survive the death of a child, and fewer survive a death by suicide. Judy and I agreed to lash ourselves to the mast and head into the heart of the storm, and we remained committed to being together when we came out on the other side. And we are now at thirty-seven years of marriage. She is my greatest strength and blessing. How I ached for what she had to endure. As the church injured me more and more deeply, she took the blows and was forced to internalize them, to the point where she began to hate the church, and my life was devoted to serving that which she was coming to despise. We searched for ways to redeem Lea's death. We participated and then became founders of a support group for those who had lost someone to suicide. We stayed in the church after the vote was taken to allow me to uphold my ministry there and after those who sought my removal had withdrawn. And we tried to go on, but the time would come for a new chapter.

36. The Police, *Reggatta de Blanc,* "Message in a Bottle"

Two years after Lea had died, we began to speak of making a move to someplace closer to family. I began to explore a new call. With each application, I was up front about Lea and about the church movement to ouster me. Most of my applications came back, *thanks, but no thanks.* I was fearful that I was seen as permanently damaged goods. One church allowed me to come all the way through to a personal visit with a committee. When they asked me to tell my story, I began and then dissolved into tears. We all knew that I was not ready or strong enough to lead a new church. More healing was to come.

Then Redeemer in Baltimore came to my awareness. This was a large church and could search nationally for its next rector. With little sense of hope, I sent them my application along with a letter describing the painful journey. For reasons unknown to me at the time, they continued in the process with me, sending requests for written materials, conducting phone interviews, and reviewing sermon recordings. Finally, a group of three came down to visit and hear me preach in person. After the service, we met in a hotel room. The interview was polite and predictable. *Tell us about how you see stewardship. Tell us about how you do adult education. Tell us about church growth.*

Finally, I said to them, "do you want to talk about Lea and about the attempt to remove me as rector here?"

They answered, "Yes."

"Were you going to bring it up?"

"No."

Well, I did. I asked for the opportunity and they welcomed the story. In the end, I asked them my most pressing question, "when you read about Lea and about the church conflict, why didn't you throw my application in the trash?"

"When we read all that, we placed your application on top."

I asked why, and they said words that will forever remain among the most redemptive I have ever heard, "because we are looking for a human being."

Healing grace washed over me at that moment, and I sensed that all would be well. Later, I would describe my call from Redeemer in this way. I was in the ocean drowning. I was going down for the third time. A supertanker came by. They threw me a life ring. They hauled me up on deck and dried me off and cared for me. Then they escorted me to the wheel house, and they pulled out the captain's chair and offered it to me.

Do I hate the church? No, but there are certainly things about the church that I hate; especially the way people can hurt other people during times of extreme pain and vulnerability. Do I love the church? Yes, but she is not always easy to love, sort of like the way we feel about the people we love. Do I forgive Lea? Yes. Lea's death has opened up to me a life I would have never known. I know about suffering in a profound way. I relate to suffering with deeper compassion. I have come to believe more deeply in resurrection, not as an abstract theological concept but as a hope so strong that all my eggs are now in that basket. I would do anything to have Lea back. What I have is the rest of my life to seek peace and to be a healer. I have a renewed sense of call to serve God and to minister to God's people, not as someone who is better than them, or morally superior to them, or as someone with deeper spiritual insight than them. Rather, I am a pilgrim traveling with other pilgrims, offering what I have and receiving what others offer me. What they offer is of immense value to me, and what I offer apparently is significant for them.

My daughter's death by suicide did not invalidate my credentials to be an ordained leader. Her death has brought me so much that what I knew before her death seems insignificant to me now. We ministers require courage and faith to be about our work. My faith comes from believing Lea is in God's care. My courage comes from experiencing God's grace sustaining me through the darkest period of my life. Insight at such a cost is something I would commend to no one, but for those of us who find ourselves on this road, it is a road of mystery and redemption. And I could never have known it were it not for Lea's death and for Lea's life.

Bibliography

Police, The. *Regatta de Blanc*. A&M Records. Originally released in 1979.

The Black Christian Church

Bishop William Young

The Healing Center, Memphis, Tennessee

The Reverend Doctor Otis Moss of Cleveland's Olivet Institutional Baptist Church once said, "Have you ever thought about the fact that, without a psychiatrist, we withstood things that send most people to the insane asylums? We didn't have the benefits of psychiatric counseling at the point of death, but the Black preacher at the funeral service became the psychiatrist, without fee. The Black Church kept the black race from committing suicide."

To a large extent, this is true. However, suicides still do occur among Black churchgoers, and we are gradually coming to address it.

The Black church experience from slavery to the present includes many denominations, Pentecostal, Baptist, Catholic, United Methodist, Mormon, and African Methodist Episcopal (AME) to name a few. Generally speaking, though not exclusively, these churches teach that the person who dies by suicide is lost spiritually for eternity, i.e., goes to hell. God is supreme, and suicide is considered to be an act against God. It is unforgivable because the person has no opportunity to repent. For many, this stigma is based on their Christian beliefs. Many preachers are uncomfortable when they have to preach at a funeral for someone who has died by suicide. They don't know what to say. They talk about everything else but the deceased. The preacher has already prejudged that the person is in hell.

The general perception in the Black community is that Black people who are in touch with their culture do not take their own lives. Suicide is considered to be a *white thing*. There is a denial that Black men take their own lives. A woman whose husband took his life formed an organization named "Black Men Don't Commit Suicide" to try to dispel this myth. A lot of these myths are hard for people to give up. A lot of these cultural mores have been passed down for generations and are very difficult to change.

Some deaths that are likely suicides are referred to as *suicide by cop*. Hopeless youth may set themselves up to be shot by police officers rather than take their own lives. Some interpret this behavior as a weakness and an inability to take responsibility, but others see these youth as trying to die with dignity. *I stood up to the cops; I am a man.* These youth know their behaviors will get them killed, but they feel like victims nonetheless. Many Black churches won't use the words *suicide, despair, hopelessness,* or *drive-by shooting.* There is a need for a different language.

Some pastors will say there is no suicide in their churches. When people need help and become suicidal, they say, the congregation comes together to pray over them, and the church takes care of the problem then and there. These pastors completely deny a role for mental health treatment and maintain that prayer alone helps people.

Fortunately, many Black congregations are beginning to see that prayer alone may not be adequate to deal with issues prevalent in the African American experience and that mental health counseling is not just a need but a necessity. Incest and child molestation, depression, unresolved grief and trauma, the effects of fatherlessness, the self-hatred of violent crime, teen mothers with illegitimate babies at an alarming rate, and the culture of silence and denial threaten the core of our society. In Tennessee, we now have a coalition among mental health societies, the state, and churches to set up community-based mental health services known as "Emotional Fitness Centers," many of which are domiciled in local churches. The Centers help prevent suicides by dealing proactively with problems such as depression and anger. In addition, churches recruit and train Peer Advocate Liaisons (PALs) to help members gain access to health care for both emotional and physical problems. We try to send a message that it is okay to care for yourself mentally, physically, and spiritually. This model has proven successful, and it is a good venue to promote total health for the African American population.

Churches are your richest resources if you can get them the right information. But in many cases, the information and the thinking need to change. Some pastors are also therapists, and an informed pastor/therapist listens rather than preaches when interacting with and individual in distress. But there is still a tremendous need to convince other pastors that both prayer and medicine are often needed to permit a person to sleep, to concentrate, and to recover from depression. This effort takes time. One of our projects in Memphis is a radio talk show with both mental health professionals and pastors that reaches a thousand people every Sunday morning. We're able to provide correct information repeatedly to our listeners. These pastors and mental health professionals have tapped into another network of around four hundred churches. Views are changing little by little, and it does take a team approach to prevent suicides.

When Someone Takes His Own Life

Reverend Norman Vincent Peale

In many ways, this seems to be the most tragic form of death. Often, the stigma of suicide is what rests most heavily on those left behind.

The Bible warns us not to judge if we ourselves hope to escape judgment, and I believe that this is the one area that biblical command especially should be heeded. For how do we know how many valiant battles such a person may have fought and won before he loses that one particular battle? And is it fair that all the good acts and impulses of such a person should be forgotten or blotted out by his final tragic act?

I think our reaction should be one of love and pity, not of condemnation. Perhaps the person was not thinking clearly in his final moments. Perhaps he was so driven by emotional whirlwinds that he was incapable of thinking at all. This is terribly sad, but surely, it is understandable. All of us have moments when we lose control of ourselves, flashes of temper or irritation or selfishness that we later regret. Each one of us, probably, has a final breaking point—or would have if our faith did not sustain us. Life puts far more pressure on some of us than it does on others. Some people have more stamina than others.

My heart goes out to those who are left behind because I know they suffer terribly. The immediate family of the victim is left wide open to tidal waves of guilt: *What did I fail to do that I should have done? What did I do that was wrong?* To such grieving persons, I can only say, *lift up your heads and your hearts. Surely, you did your best, and surely the loved one who is gone did his best for as long as he could. Remember, now, that his battles and torments are over. Do not judge him, and do not presume to fathom the mind of God where this one of his children is concerned.*

A few years ago, when a young man died by his own hand, a service for him was conducted by his pastor, the Reverend West Stephens. What he said that day expresses far more eloquently than I can the message that I'm trying to convey. Here are some of his words:

"Our friend died on his own battlefield. He was killed in action fighting a civil war. He fought against adversaries that were as real to him as his casket is real to us. They were powerful adversaries. They took toll of his energies and endurance. They exhausted the last vestiges of his courage and his strength. At last, these adversaries overwhelmed him, and it appeared that he had lost the war. But did he? I see a host of victories that he has won!

"For one thing, he has won our admiration because even if he lost the war, we give him credit for his bravery on the battlefield, and we give him credit for the courage and pride and hope that he used as his weapons as long as he could. We shall remember not his death but his daily victories gained through his kindnesses and thoughtfulness, through his love for his family and friends, for all things beautiful, lovely, and honorable. We shall remember not his last day of defeat, but we shall remember the many days that he was victorious over overwhelming odds. We shall remember not the years we thought he had left but the intensity with which he lived the years that he had. Only God knows what this child of his suffered in the silent skirmishes that took place in his soul, but our consolation is that God does know and understands."

Bibliography

Peale, Norman Vincent. *The Healing of Sorrow.* Pawling, NY: Inspirational Book Service; Distributed to the Book Trade by Doubleday, Garden City, N.Y., 1966.

Chapter Five

Resources, Order of Service, Music, etc.

∾

An Interfaith Worship Service

REVEREND JAMES T. CLEMONS

Used at the National Interfaith Conference On Religion And Suicide
April 5, 2000
Cecil B. Day Chapel the Carter Center
Atlanta, Georgia

Opening Dialogue (responsively):

If it had not been the Lord who was on our side,
then the flood would have swept us away,
the torrent would have gone over us;
then the raging waters would have gone over us.
Our help is in the name of the Lord,
who made heaven and earth.

Hymn: Our God, Our Help, Isaac Watts, 1719; alt.

Opening Prayer (unison):

Gracious God:

accept the praise and prayers of your people.
Let the words of our mouths
and the meditations of our hearts
be acceptable in your sight, O Lord,
our rock and our redeemer. Amen.

Psalm 69:13–18

Psalm 130

Litany

O God, from of old, those in distress have cried to you, seeking your help and deliverance in the time of despair. We remember those who even now cry out to you for help because they have found no hope here.
Receive their prayer and rescue them.
For all those who have come to know that you have answered them, for all who have stepped back from the edge of the abyss because of your love.
We give you thanks.
We remember those who did not find hope in this life, who have ended their earthly existence rather than endure its darkness.
To you we commend them, gracious God.
Let your light perpetual shine upon them.
We intercede also for those who have been left behind in sorrow and frustration, bearing heavy burdens of guilt, even for things they could not have changed, and placing blame on others.
Have mercy on them, O God. Grant them the assurance
of your goodness, and pour out your kindness upon them.
Give wisdom and patience to those who provide counsel for suicidal persons,
for their families and all who love them
Enable them to speak the proper word in its season,
and let their work bear much good fruit.
Teach us how best we may minister to such as these for whom we pray, to give encouragement and hope, to be examples of graciousness and understanding.
Work in us to transform our own hearts,
and work through us for the sake of those to whom we minister.

Great is your name, O God,
and greatly to be praised.
Blessed are you, sovereign of the universe
and savior of your people. Amen.

Hymn

When in sadness lost and grieving—Alfred Chiplin, 2000

Dismissal with Blessing

Go forth in hope and confidence.
Be strong and of good courage.
Do not be afraid or dismayed, for God is your strength.
The Lord bless you and keep you.
The Lord let his face shine upon you, and be gracious to you.
The Lord look upon you kindly and give you peace, now and always.
Amen.[1]

Four Candles for Moving Forward

We light this candle in honor and in memory of those we love who have died so suddenly. We are reminded of their special presence in our lives. We remember the light times, the times of togetherness. We recall the dark times and the times of struggle. Most of all we remember that our loved ones continue to be and will continue to be a part of us.

We light a second candle, acknowledging the pain of grief. We know that our pain is very very deep. We know that as we move along life's road, the pain will soften but will always be with us.

The third candle is lit in hope. Just as the flame of the candle pierces the darkness, so *hope* gradually returns to light and illuminate our way.

The fourth candle is lit in love. Knowing that love does not die, it remains with us and so will those we remember today, always be a part of us forever and ever.

Invite loved ones to come forward and light a candle from one of the four candles. Allow them to mention the name of the deceased.

---

1. Numbers 6:24–26

Celebrating the Life and New Life of N____
Date of birth through date of death

Diann L. Neu

Preparation

Choose a place for this service that is appropriate for the family, a church, home, backyard, by water, or space that is meaningful for the mourners. Place a table in the center of a circle of chairs and cover it with a cloth—perhaps a shawl or clothing that belonged to N____—a candle on a candlestick that belonged to N____, and an object that symbolizes freedom for N____.

The following objects have been used in wakes, funerals, and burials: flowers, earth, water with floating flowers, herbs, leaves, oils, salt, salt water, oil, bread, an open bird cage, hands, rocks, stones, shells, children's toys, material with knots that will be untied at some point. Meaningful rituals have included planting a tree, watching stars or the moon, releasing balloons, butterflies, or doves, and burning candles or incense.

Invite family members and friends to participate if they wish. For example, several could read a line each of the "Litany of Remembrance" below. Add music as appropriate for the group gathered. Have a packet of forget-me-not seeds for each person.

Music Prelude

Welcome

(Names of the immediate family members) and their families welcome you to this service of thanksgiving for the life of N____. We gather to remember her, to tell stories about how we knew her, and to bid her farewell. We come together to support her loved ones and one another in our sorrow. (The partner or spouse), we thank you for being N's beloved partner and accompanying her through life and death into a new life. (Name the children), we thank you for honoring your mother.

Lighting the Memorial Candle

(Invite a child to light the candle from the candlestick of N____)

119

We light this candle to remember N___, (add the words that describe her, e.g., wife and life partner, mother, grandmother, daughter, friend, cousin, elder of the extended family, colleague, mentor, nurse, enjoyer of music, world traveler, intellectual inquirer, lover of music, struggler to find meaning in life, seeker of justice, etc.).

Reading

Use a reading that reflects the spirit of N___. Before or after it, interact with the symbol. For example, open the bird cage and make reference to the spirit of N___ being set free.

Psalm 121

Song

(Sing a favorite song of N___'s or a song that comforts the family) "How Can I Keep from Singing," early Quaker song, American gospel tune, in *Singing the Living Tradition*, Beacon Press, 1993.

The Life of N___

Give a brief bio of N___ and share photos or video of her life.

N___ died on (give date and an account something like what follows). Her spirit had been deteriorating over the past few months. She could no longer keep going on her journey upon Earth.

N___ made choices we may not agree with, but we all make choices as part of being human. She lived on the edge. She struggled to make sense of life, and she died of her own choice. Her death surprised us. It was out of season. The impact of its suddenness, the unimaginable reasons, the implied insult of being so suddenly left behind, the questions and more questions leave us with a great mixture of emotions.

Yet today, we are here to celebrate N___'s life and to affirm our conviction that death is not the end. It is but one more step in life's path. Our faith tells us that nothing can separate us from the love of God, the Divine Holy One. Nothing can separate N___ from the love of God. May God's love and the strength of our friendship support each of us.

Sharing Memories of N___

We all have memories of N___. A few of her family and friends would like to share stories now. (Sharing) Take a minute in silence to remember her. (Pause) Later on tonight or tomorrow, share this special memory with one of the family, if you wish.

(Close with) Let us join hands in a moment of silence to feel N___'s presence with us and wish her peace. (Pause) Let us let go of our hands and let go of her as we have known her.

Song

Choose a memorable closing song, perhaps "Amazing Grace."

Burial Ideas

- Fill a clay vessel with earth from the birth place of N___ and place her ashes in it or pour the earth over her casket.

- Choose papers or objects to bury with the body or ashes like photos, a letter, a favorite CD, a teddy bear.

- Place a stone on the grave and ask forgiveness for any injustice you may have done to N___.

- Plant a tree, flowers, or bulbs over an earthen grave.

- Launch a balloon or balloons as a symbol of resurrection. (avoid mylar balloons, which are a hazard to the environment).

- Release doves as a symbol of resurrection.

- Ring or toll bells, sound chimes, or play a bagpipe.

- Release butterflies as a symbol of transformation. You can purchase monarchs at Bird's Butterflies (734.731.6686, www.birdsbutterflies. com) or buy cocoons at a science store.

- Gather water from a lake, ocean, stream, or river that N___ enjoyed and use it in the memorial.

- Scatter the cremated ashes with rose petals into the sea.

Commitment of Ashes (Or Body)

We commit N___'s ashes back to water, the essence of all of our lives (or her body to the earth by planting a tree and putting the ashes around it). In this single moment of eternity, we stand collectively before you, Divine Holy One, and call upon our angels, specifically N___'s (name ancestors like mother, father, and others) and all those precious unnamed souls to be present, as we commit N___'s earthly remains to the oceans (or the earth).

Our God and our angles, we commit N___'s ashes (body) to this ocean (earth), so that she may continue her travels through this world. We commit her soul to your loving care. We commit her spirit to our hearts and to the hearts of those she loved and who love her. Our beloved N___, we humbly and ever so lovingly set you free (Scatter the ashes or put earth on the body. All put shells or flowers in the water or the earth).

Litany of Remembrance

A wonderful piece of poetry, "We Remember Them," by Sylvan Kamens and Rabbi Jack Riemer, can be inserted here and modified for the particular person.

Extinguishing the Memorial Candle

(Blow out the candle)

The light and spirit of N___'s life no longer burns through her physical body, but it will continue to burn in the hearts of all who cherish her memory.

Closing Blessing

"She Whom We Love" by St. John Chrysostom

Greeting of Peace

Let us close our time together by offering one another a greeting of peace and exchanging packets of forget-me-not seeds with one another. Let us send one another forth, exchanging the seeds and saying: "Peace and healing be with you" (Exchange seeds).

Sending Forth

As we go into the future, may healing flow from sorrow, may hope emerge from darkness, and may love which is stronger than death sustain our spirits and give us peace this day and always. May N___ rest in peace. Amen. Blessed be. Let it be so.

Reference

Kamens, Sylvans and Rabbi Jack Riemer. "We Remember Them." *Shiva.com.* http://www.shiva.com/learning-center/resources/poems-of-comfort/#remem

Healing Memorial

REVEREND C. KAREN COVEY-MOORE AND ANNE CRONIN TYSON, MA

We come from many faiths, many religions.

We call a higher power by many names—Yahweh, Allah, God, Jesus, the Great Spirit, and many more.

We each come with a story. Each Story is a Sacred Story. When we come together to share them, this becomes a Sacred Place—Holy Ground.

Some of you come so crushed in spirit that you can no longer believe in a loving being.

Believe in the gathered love present here tonight in your fellow loved ones.

Believe in the light shining forth tonight in spite of the darkness that we have experienced that threatened to extinguish our own light.

Believe in the spirit and hope that springs forth deep within us from a place we don't fully know yet as we look to our brothers and sisters who have endured, survived, and moved forward.

There is one love—one light—one Spirit of the universe that sustains us.

Tonight we come together in that one love—One Light.

Our loved ones are a part of that light. They brought a light to the world,

and we can choose to carry that light of our loved one forward into the world.

In silence now, we reflect on the light that our loved one brought into our lives and to the world around them. When you are ready, please come forward, say their name—perhaps you might want to mention a word that describes their special light that you would like to carry forward into the world for them—and then light their candle.

Play "Light A Candle."

After all candles are lit and all are gathered up front, ask those who have lost a loved one five or more years ago to step to the right side and those five years or less to step to the left. Alternately, ask those who are five years or fewer survivors return to their seats and those five or more years remain up front. Once seated, have the five-year plus each take tapers and go out to those seated and light the taper from the candle and hand it to the survivor (do this after the song). When all are lit, the leader says, "Together," etc.

Play "Who Will Come and Share My Sorrow." This could be played after the first group has returned to their seats or before. The loved ones on the right will come forward and light a taper from a votive candle in the person's hand and hand them the taper.

After tapers are lit.

Leader: Together, we will walk.

Together, we will survive.

Together, we will bear the light of our loved ones to the world to light and illuminate the darkness.

Leader: We invite you to blow out your candles for the time being but light them often to remember the light you bear.

Final blessing. Some exchange of peace between the loved ones.

Items needed:

- Votive candles
- Tapers

[Somewhere in the service, long-term survivors might offer a word of advice as to how they managed to get through each day.—Ed.]

∽

Resources from the United Methodist Book of Worship
For an Untimely or Tragic Death

Words of Grace and Sentences

Blessed be the God who consoles us in all our affliction,
so that we may be able to console those who are in any affliction
with the consolation
with which we ourselves are consoled by God. (2 Cor 1:3a, 4).
Cast your burden on the Lord, and God will sustain you. (Ps 55:22a, alt.).

Prayers

Jesus our Friend, you wept at the grave of Lazarus,
you know all our sorrows.
Behold our tears, and bind up the wounds of our hearts.
Through the mystery of pain,
Bring us into closer communion with you and with one another.
Raise us from death into life.
And grant, in your mercy, that with *Name*, who has passed within the veil,
we may come to live, with you and with all whom we love,
in our Father's home. *Amen.*
God of us all, we thank you for Christ's grace,
Through which we pray to you in this dark hour.
A life we love has been torn from us.
Expectations the years once held have vanished.
The mystery of death has stricken us.
O God, you know the lives we live and the deaths we die-
woven so strangely of purpose and of chance,
of reason and of the irrational,
of strength and of frailty, of happiness and of pain.
into your hands we commend the soul of *Name*.
No mortal life you have made is without eternal meaning.
No earthly fate is beyond your redeeming.

Through your grace that can do far more than we can think or imagine,
fulfill in *Name* your purpose that reaches beyond time and death.
Lead *Name* from strength to strength,
and fit *Name* for love and service in your kingdom.
Into your hands also we commit our lives.
You alone, God, make us to dwell in safety.
Whom, finally, have we on earth or in heaven but you?
Help us to know the measure of our days, and how frail we are.
Hold us in you keeping. Forgive us our sins.
Save our minds from despair and our hearts from fear.
And guard and guide us with your peace. *Amen.*
Ever living God, in Christ's resurrection
you turned the disciples' despair into triumph, their sorrow into joy.
Give us faith to believe that every good that seems to be overcome by evil,
and every love that seems to be buried in death,
shall rise again to life eternal;
through Jesus Christ, who lives and reigns with you for ever more. *Amen.*
Almighty God, in your keeping there is shelter from the storm,
and in your mercy there is comfort for the sorrows of life.
Hear now our prayer for those who mourn and our heavy laden.
Give to them strength to bear and do your will.
Lighten their darkness with your love.
Enable them to see beyond the things of this mortal world
the promise of the eternal.
Help them to know that your care enfolds all your people,
that you are our refuge and strength,
and that underneath are your everlasting arms. *Amen.*

Scripture Readings

Lamentations 3:19–26, 31–33	Remember my affliction. God is good.
Psalm 103 (UMH 824)	Bless the Lord, who redeems from death.
Revelation 21:1–6; 22:1–5	God will wipe away every tear.
See Canticle of Hope (UMH 734)	
Mark 4:35–41	Jesus' calming of the storm
Luke 15:11–32	The prodigal son
John 6:35–40	God's will that nothing be lost

Suggested Hymns from UMH

534	Be Still, My Soul
528	Nearer, My God, to Thee
557	Blest Be the Tie That Binds
117	O God, Our Help in Ages Past
141	Children of the Heavenly Father
480	O Love That Wilt Not Let Me Go
510	Come, Ye Disconsolate
474	Precious Lord, Take My Hand
129	Give to the Winds Thy Fears
356	*Pues Si Vivimos* (When We are Living; esp. for a young adult)
128	He Leadeth Me: O Blessed Thought
707	Hymn of Promise (especially for a youth)
308	Thine Be the Glory (especially for a middle adult)
452	My Faith Looks Up to Thee
525	We'll Understand It Better By and By

Other

Prayers

Almighty God, our Father, from whom we come,
and to whom our spirits return:
You have been our dwelling place in all generations.
You are our refuge and strength, a very present help in trouble.
Grant us your blessing in this hour,
and enable us so to put our trust in you
that our spirits may grow calm and our hearts be comforted.
Lift our eyes beyond the shadows of earth,
and help us to see the light of eternity.
So may we find grace and strength for this and every time of need;
through Jesus Christ our Lord. *Amen.*

Scripture Readings

Genesis 15:15	Abraham's death
Genesis 49:1, 29–33; 50:1–2, 12–14	Jacob's death and Joseph's response
Exodus 15 (UMH 135)	Canticle of Moses and Miriam
Joshua 3:14—4:7	Crossing over Jordan
Job 1:21	Job's faith
Job 14:1–12a	We are of few days.
Job 19:25–27	My Redeemer lives.
Proverbs 31:10–13, 19–20, 30–31	A good woman
Isaiah 25:1,6–9	God will swallow up death.
Isaiah 26:1–4, 19	Your dead shall live.
Isaiah 35:1–6,10	Zion restored
Isaiah 41:8–10, 13	Do not fear.
Isaiah 57:14–19	Poem of consolation
Isaiah 61:1–4, 10–11	The Spirit of the Lord is upon me.
Isaiah 66:10–13	As a mother comforts, so does God
Ezekiel 34:11–16	Shepherd of Israel
Ezekiel 37:1–14, 21–28	These bones can live.
Micah 6:6–8	What does the Lord require?
Zephaniah 3:16–20	Restoration of Israel
Psalm 27 (UMH 758)	Devotion and deliverance
Psalm 34 (UMH 769)	Thanksgiving for deliverance
Psalm 40 (UMH 774)	Thanksgiving for deliverance
Psalm 71 (UMH 794)	Deliverance from evil
Psalm 77 (UMH 798)	Deliverance from trouble
Psalm 84 (UMH 804)	How Lovely is your dwelling place.
Psalm 118 (UMH 839)	Thanksgiving for deliverance
Psalm 126 (UMH 847)	Prayer for deliverance
Psalm 143 (UMH 856)	Prayer for deliverance
Acts 10:34–43	Peter's sermon on Jesus' resurrection
Romans 5:1–11, 17–21	Peace with God through faith

Romans 6:3–11	Dying and rising with Christ
Romans 14:7–9	Christ, Lord of the dead and the living
2 Corinthians 5:1–11a, 14–20	Away from the body, at home in the Lord
Ephesians 3:14–21	Bow before God; know the love of Christ
Philippians 3:7–21	The power of Christ's resurrection
Colossians 3:1–17	Raised with Christ
1 Thessalonians 4:13—5:11	Concerning those who sleep
2 Timothy 4:6–8, 17–18	I have fought the good fight
Hebrews 11—12	The saints of God
1 John 3:1–3	We shall be like God.
Revelation 14:1–3, 6–7, 12–13	Blessed are the dead in the Lord.
Matthew 5:1–12	The Beatitudes
Matthew 6:19–21	Do not lay up treasures on Earth.
Matthew 11:25–30	Come to me all who labor.
Matthew 25:31–46	As you did it to one of the least
Matthew 28:1–10, 16–20	Jesus' resurrection: go make disciples
Mark 16:1–8	The open tomb: Jesus goes before you.
Luke 1:67–75 (UMH 208)	Canticle of Zechariah
Luke 12:22–40	Do not be anxious; be ready.
Luke 24:1–12	The empty tomb
John 3:13–17	God's gift of eternal life
John 5:19–29	Whoever hears and believes has life.
John 6:30–40, 47–51	Jesus, the bread of life
John 10:1–18, 27–30	Jesus, the Good Shepherd
John 12:20–36	Unless a grain of wheat dies
John 15:1–17	The vine and the branches
John 16:12–22, 33	Sorrow becomes joy.
John 20	Jesus' resurrection

Suggested Hymns from UMH

See Hymns 700–707 Death and Eternal Life and 708–712 Communion of the Saints. Also, see suggestions under Eternal Life and Funerals and Memorial Services in UMH 940–42 and the following:

163	Ask Ye What Great Thing I Know
557	Blest Be the Tie that Binds
141	Children of the Heavenly Father
318	Christ Is Alive
407	Close to Thee
709	Come, Let us Join Our Friends Above (stanzas 3, 4)
491	Remember Me
510	Come, Ye Disconsolate
315	Come, Ye Faithful, Raise the Strain
710	Faith of Our Fathers
129	Give to the Winds Thy Fears
654	How Blest Are They (for an older adult)
703	Swing Low, Sweet Chariot
77	How Great Thou Art
103	Immortal, Invisible, God Only Wise
314	In The Garden (stanzas 1, 5)
488	Jesus, Remember Me
133	Leaning On The Everlasting Arms (stanzas 1, 5)
59	Mil Voces Para Celebrar (O For a Thousand Voices to Sing)
303	The Day of Resurrection
520	Nobody Knows the Trouble I See
57	O For a Thousand Tongues to Sing
143	On Eagle's Wings
773	Marching to Zion
368	My Hope is Built
356	Pues Si Vivimos (When We Are Living)
66	Praise, My Soul, The King of Heaven
523	Saranam, Saranam (Refuge)
666	Shalom to you
512	Stand by Me
704	Steal Away to Jesus
496	Sweet Hour of Prayer
395	Take Time To Be Holy
545	The Church's One Foundation
546	The Church's One Foundation

Bibliography

The United Methodist Book of Worship. Nashville, TN. The United Methodist Publishing House, 1992. (Permission granted)

Serving Jewish Families of Suicide
Helping Them Make Their Memories a Blessing In the Midst of Tragedy, Anger, Shame and Guilt, Part II

Thoughts from Two Rabbi Survivors of Family Suicide

Rabbis Chaya Gusfield and Lori Klein

Accompanying and Giving Voice to the Family

Funeral

We should treat the funeral after a suicide as a vital moment in an ongoing pastoral relationship, whether we expect to remain in contact with the surviving family members or not. The funeral will become a touchstone of memory, either helping or hindering the family's healing from this collective and individual trauma. Handled carelessly, the funeral itself can become a source of shame or pain as family and friends struggle to make meaning from the suicide. Handled well, the funeral can help counteract the inevitably unhelpful or harmful remarks others will make to the family. At best, family members can feel so accompanied in their myriad feelings at the funeral, they can begin to integrate this tragedy into their life's journey in a meaningful and life-giving manner.

A familiar array of prayers and readings often appear in funerals. Prayers families may find particularly helpful are Psalm 121 (I lift my eyes to the heavens, from where does my help come?), Psalm 147:3 (G-d as Healer of the brokenhearted), and, of course, Psalm 23. All of these psalms share the theme of connection with the Divine, which may be helpful in countering suicide survivors' sense of isolation and their fear that no one can understand their particular misery. Many people find the line in Psalm 23 which says, "my cup runs over," to be jarring and incongruous with the mood of the beginning of that psalm. After any death, particularly after a suicide, we are not likely to view our lives as overflowing with joy or contentment. This verse can be reframed as a statement to G-d that our cup sometimes feels too full, too full of sorrow, pain, or trouble. We ask G-d for a bigger cup, to somehow give us the increased capacity to bear what seems impossible to bear.

Other standard funeral prayers are less useful, particularly Ecclesiastes 3:1–8 (to everything there is a season) and the statement that "Adonai has given, Adonai has taken, blessed be the name of Adonai."[2] The clergy person's custom or interpretation of Jewish law may lead her or him to feel compelled to use one or both of these pieces. If so, we should think carefully about how to introduce or comment on them to minimize the special pain mourners may feel hearing these words after a suicide. For example, we can acknowledge these prayers sound hollow, false, or even painful, and then talk about the wisdom that comes from reflecting on the meaning of our traditional prayers. In this setting, these prayers remind us we are not in control of the timing of our loved one's death, regardless of its cause. Another approach is to use a creative English translation of the Hebrew line from Job 1:21 (*Adonai natan*, etc.). For example, Rabbi Eli Cohen of Santa Cruz translates that line in this way, "Out of the mystery, we come and into the mystery we go. Through it all, we bless the source of life for the gift of life."

Hesped (Eulogy)

Unlike other funerals, we must decide whether to give a eulogy, or *hesped*, at all. Traditional Jewish legal sources forbid the use of *hesped* at the funeral of an "intentional" suicide.[3] As Abraham Zevi Eisenstadt, author of *Pitchei Teshuva* said, "We mourn, but we do not eulogize." The primary reason cited for omitting a *hesped* is the eulogy serves to honor the deceased.[4] In some circumstances, giving no *hesped* at all might be the best compromise for a family in strong conflict about what to say in a *hesped*. Also, for some families, the belief that not eulogizing the deceased might hasten the atonement of their loved one's soul may have spiritual resonance for them. However, we should take great care when deciding to omit a *hesped* to ensure surviving family members do not leave the funeral with a burden of shame or have that feeling accentuated.

There is also a minority opinion for giving a *hesped*, even in the case of an "intentional" suicide. In the early eighteenth century, a German rabbi,

2. Job 1:21

3. *Shulchan Aruch, Yore Deah* 345:1

4. Babylonian Talmud, *Sanhedrin* 46b–47a and Rashi commentary on those pages

Ezekiel Katzenellenbogen, cited Rashi for the proposition there is no one in Israel who does not have within him or her *Torah* and *mitzvot*. While Katzenellenbogen was not ruling on suicide, he used Saul, who killed himself yet was entitled to be properly eulogized, as a supporting argument for his ruling. Progressive legal authorities, such as responsa from the Reform movement, cite Katzenellenbogen as justification for giving a *hesped* at the funeral for someone who has died by suicide.[5]

The *hesped* can be a powerful inspiration for surviving friends and family to begin to make meaning of their loved one's suicide.

Bibliography

Jacob, Walter, ed. "American Reform Responsa: Collected Responsa of the Central Conference of American Rabbis 1889–1983." New York: CCAR, 1983, 299–307

5. American Reform Reponsa, 299–307

Service of Death and Resurrection for a Seminary Student
December 6, 1989

JAMES T. CLEMONS, PHD
Wesley Theological Seminary

Gathering

Musical Voluntaries

Word of Welcome: President of the Seminary

> *The United Methodist service of Death and Resurrection begins on page 880 of The United Methodist Hymnal.*

Entrance

The Word of Grace: *All who are able, please stand.*

United Methodist Book of Worship 871

Anthem: *Give rest, O Christ, to your servant with your saints,*

(Words: Eastern Orthodox Memorial Service. Tr. *The Book of Common Prayer*, 1979. Music: *Kontakion (Kievan chant)*, From Eastern Orthodox Memorial Service)

Greeting: United Methodist Hymnal 871

Hymn: "The Strife is o'er, the Battle Done" Victory

Prayer: Seated United Methodist Hymnal 871

Proclamation and Response

Song: "Fire and Rain," James Taylor

Scriptures

A reading from the book of Lamentations (Lamentations 3:22–24, 31–33)

> (The Lord is all I have, and so in God I put my hope.)

The favors of the Lord are not exhausted, his mercies are not spent; they are renewed each morning, so great is his faithfulness. My portion is the Lord, says my soul, therefore I will hope in him. For the Lord's rejection does not last forever; though he punishes, he takes pity, in the abundance of his mercies. He has no joy in afflicting or grieving the sons of men.
This is the Word of the Lord.
All respond: Thanks be to God.

A reading from the book of Job.(Job 19:23–27)

(But in my heart, I know that my Redeemer lives.)
Oh, would that my words were written down! Would that they were inscribed in a record: That with an iron chisel and with lead they were cut in the rock forever! But as for me, I know that my Vindicator lives, and that he will at last stand forth upon the dust; Whom I myself shall see: my own eyes, not another's, shall behold him.
This is the Word of the Lord.
All respond: Thanks be to God.

Psalm 23 (in unison) United Methodist Hymnal 754, Response 1

A reading from the letter of Paul to the Romans (Romans 14:7–9).

(Whether therefore we live or die, we belong to the Lord.)
None of us lives as his own master and none of us dies as his own master. While we live we are responsible to the Lord, and when we die we die his servants. Both in life and in death we are the Lord's. That is why Christ died and came to life again, that he might be Lord of both the dead and the living.
This is the Word of the Lord.
All respond: Thanks be to God.

A reading from the letter of Paul to the Romans (Romans 6:3–4, 8).

(If we have died with Christ, we shall live with him.)
Are you not aware that we who were baptized into Jesus Christ were baptized into his death? Through baptism into his death, we were buried with him, so that, just as Christ was raised from the dead by the glory of the father, we too might live a new life. If we have died with Christ, we believe that we are also to live with him.
This is the Word of the Lord.
All respond: Thanks be to God.

A reading from the book of Revelation. (Revelation 14:13)

(Blessed are those who die in the Lord.)
And I heard a voice from heaven say to me: "Write this down: Happy now are the dead who die in the Lord!" The Spirit added, Yes, they shall find rest from their labors, for their good works accompany them."
This is the Word of the Lord.
All respond: Thanks be to God.

A reading from the book of John (John 11:21–27).

(I am the resurrection, and I am Life.)
Martha said to Jesus: "Lord, if you had been here, my brother would never have died. Even now, I am sure that God will give you whatever you ask of him." "Your brother will rise again," Jesus assured her. "I know he will rise again," Martha replied, "in the resurrection on the last day." Jesus told her, "I am the resurrection and the life: whoever believes in me, though he should die, will come to life; and whoever is alive and believes in me will never die. Do you believe this?" "Yes, Lord," she replied. "I have come to believe that you are the Messiah, the Son of God: he who is to come into this world."
This is the Word of the Lord.
All respond: Thanks be to God.

A reading from the book of Romans (Romans 8:31, 33–35, 37–39).

(If God is on our side, who is against us? Nothing in all creation can separate us from the love of God in Christ Jesus.)
If God is for us, who can be against us? Who shall bring a charge against God's chosen ones? God, who justifies? Who shall condemn them? Christ Jesus, who died or rather was raised up, who is at the right hand of God and who intercedes for us? Who will separate us from the love of Christ? Trial or distress, or persecution, or hunger, of nakedness, or danger, or the sword? Yet in all this we are more than conquerors because of him who has loved us. For I am certain that neither death nor life, neither angels nor principalities, neither the present nor the future nor powers, neither height nor depth nor any other creature, will be able to separate us from the love of God that comes to us in Jesus Christ.
This is the Word of the Lord.
All respond: Thanks be to God.

137

Sermon

Response from the Family

Hymn: "What Wondrous Love is This"

Commendation: United Methodist Hymnal 874–875

Exchanging the Peace of Christ

Offertory

Thanksgiving and Communion

Word and Table III: United Methodist Hymnal 15–16

Eucharistic music: "Sanctus C" United Methodist Hymnal 21
Music during the communion:
"On Eagle's Wings"
"Here I am, Lord"
"When We All Get to Heaven"

Prayer of Thanksgiving: United Methodist Hymnal 875

In Paradisum

Into paradise may the angels lead you.
At your coming may the martyrs receive you,
and bring you into the holy city Jerusalem.
May the choirs of angels welcome you,
and with Lazarus who once was poor
may you have peace everlasting.

Closing Hymn: Christ the Victorious" United Methodist Hymnal 653 Russian Hymn

Dismissal with Blessing

Chapter Six

Imagery and Ideas to Set the Emotional Tone

If you have a good metaphor, poem, or story in mind, it is so much easier to start writing your sermon or eulogy. In this chapter, we share some imagery that might spark your thought pattern. These devices, metaphors, simile, poems, Biblical quotes, and parables, can not only leave lasting impressions but possibly might also mitigate a sense of responsibility for family and friends of someone who died by their own hand. All of these vehicles are powerful tools which we should not overlook.

First, let us review some powerful literary tools:

a) *Metaphor*, a figure of speech which makes an implicit, implied, or hidden comparison between two things or objects that are poles apart from each other but have some characteristics common between them. For example, you will travel through a "canyon of whys"[1] as you struggle to find some sort of relief for this death, or he drowned in a sea of grief. A metaphor does not use *as* and *like*, as does a simile. Ask people to use a metaphor to describe their feelings, and you will realize new insight as to where they are in the grieving process. Use metaphor in your speech, and people will relate to the imagery by using their own life experiences.

b) *Simile*, a figure of speech that compares two things that are alike in some way. A simile uses the words *like* and *as* to make the comparison clearer. A good example illustrating the mystery of why one person

---

1. A metaphor provided by Frank R. Campbell, Ph.D., LCSW, C.T in his unpublished manuscript "The Canyon of Why: Metaphors for Healing from Sudden and Traumatic Loss."

dies before others might be that the deceased is like the one rose in a bouquet that dies before the others. Giving the bouquet is not lessened by experiencing the loss of a single rose. Though the bouquet now is a little less full, we can remember the smell and the beauty of the lost flower, just as we remember the beauty of our deceased.

c) Poetry and parables are voices that resonate with people's emotional experience in a deeply meaningful and transformational way. The term *parable* in its Greek origin means, *to place or cast things side by side*. Thus, a parable compares two things. Amy-Jill Levine writes in her book *The Misunderstood Jew*, "Parables seek to arrest the listeners, to show another perspective on the world, to call into question the status quo. They often convey news that audiences do not want to hear, and yet, they do so in ways that may bring a smile through wild exaggeration, ridiculous scenarios, and startling juxtapositions."[2]

Below, you will find a small sample of materials that might stimulate your creative juices. We encourage you to search the web for grief poems, poems of comfort, or poems for suicidal deaths. You will find a myriad that might be a special hook upon which to hang your eulogy. Below are just a few examples that we liked.

❧

For a Younger Person

> We can't know why the lily
> has so brief a time to bloom
> In the warmth of
> sunlight's kiss upon its face
> Before it folds it fragrance in
> And bids the world goodnight
> To rest its beauty in a gentler place.
> But we can know that nothing that is loved
> is ever lost,
> And no one who has ever touched a heart
> can really pass away
> Because some beauty lingers

2. Levine, *The Misunderstood Jew,* 34

In each memory
of which they've been a part.

– Ellen Brenneman[3]

A Prayer

—May all that which my life raised up—
these works, these loves—
hold firm a time beyond my passing.
May they nourish other lives
as others nourished mine,
give scope for new beginnings.
And in the end,
when the music of my life
fades in the earth like an echo,
may all those who held me
in their words or arms
let me pass
into them,
    through them,
and fall back among the living.

– Robert Neimeyer (permission granted)

3. Anderson, *First Tears*, 84

Dear Brian

Dear Brian—
No one seemed to notice
What you were going through;
We all just kept on seeing
The man we wanted to.
If we did not see
The pain that you were in
Or ask, or offer help
Forgive us for that sin.
Now we know your worries
Crease your brow no more
And your spirit rests in peace
Upon that distant shore.
And we in turn remember
The good times, not the bad:
We remember when you laughed with us,
Not when you were sad.
And laugh—we laughed often
For good times there were plenty
With jokes and songs and beer and wine
And a glass that was never empty
Like all the best friendships
Most valued when you win them,
Our lives have been the richer
Because you have been in them.
Good-bye, Brian, God Bless and Godspeed.

     – Author Unknown

Toward Fields of Light

To have made one soul
the better for one's birth.

To have added but one flower
To the garden of the earth;
To have struck one blow for truth
In the daily fight with lies;
To have done one deed of right
In the face of calumnies;
To have sown in the souls of humankind
One thought that will not die-
To have been a link in the chain of life
Shall be immortality.

– Edwin Hatch[4]

Thus, Eden becomes the paradise that we have lost. We no longer have peace with the world. We are no longer whole, we are broken. One lesson (Eli) Wiesel derives from the Garden of Eden story is that, though expelled from paradise, Adam and Eve did not give in to resignation. In the face of death, they decided to fight by giving life, by conferring a meaning on life . . . Their children would die—never mind! One moment of life contains eternity . . . Though defeated by God, he [Adam] did not wallow in self denial . . . When God created man, God gave him a secret—and that secret was not how to begin but how to begin again . . . and he [man] does so every time he chooses to defy death and side with the living. Thus, he justifies the ancient plan of the most ancient of men, Adam, to whom we are bound both by the anguish that oppressed him and the defiance that elevated him above the paradise we shall never enter.
. . . As Wiesel puts it: "Every one of us yearns to recapture some lost paradise, every one of us bears the mark of some violated stolen innocence." To turn away from death and begin again is a lesson I wish many of my contemporaries could hear.[5]

– Benjamin Edidin Scolnic[6]

4. Hatch, *A Jewish Service During Shiva*, 20
5. Downing, *Elie Wiesel: A Religious Biography*.
6. Midstream, August/September 1992, 32–33.

Image: A Boat Tossed Upon Rough Seas

No matter how firm the rigging or deep the hull,
a ship sometimes becomes a fragile vessel amid raging storms.
We survive in a vale of tears,
beneath a cloud of uncertainty.
"Whys" and "if onlys" give us no rest.
Yet, in our searching we find certitude.
The ending of this precious life was not right
for this beloved, and was not right for us.
When our boat seems so small,
the waves so large,
we must find a better port than this.
For this loved one, the enemy Death
poured through. But it is not for us
to judge defenses that did not hold.
And what of God?
Our Creator is surely strong enough
to pick up the pieces of self-ended lives.
Will our God,
who marks the sparrow's course,
judge life by one moment of ending
or by the rowing of a lifetime?

    – William John Fitzgerald[7]

7. Fitzgerald, *Words of Comfort*

Prayer for the Deceased

The turbulent waves have ceased, O God. Bring our dear journeyer to a tranquil shore. May an eternal tide of peace wash over this troubled traveler's soul.

– William John Fitzgerald[8]

Some people come into our lives and quickly go.

Some move our souls to dance. They awaken us to new understanding with the passing whisper of their wisdom.

Some people make the sky more beautiful to gaze upon. They stay in our lives for a while, leave footprints on our hearts, and we are never, ever the same.

– Flavia Weedn[9]

Logotherapist Viktor Frankl wrote, "It matters little whether a person performs much or little, as long as he/she performs his/her tasks as he/she honestly sees it, to the best of his/her abilities and responsibleness."

"Life is not measured by the number of breaths we take, but by the moments that take our breath away."

– Vicki Corona[10]

8. Ibid.
9. *Flavia and the Dream Maker*
10. *Tahitian Choreographies*

I would hope I've done well—that my lifetime record shows Me a giver—not a taker.—(Reports someone who knows.)

Hopefully lighten hearts—created laughter and light ... With efforts sincere, sought poor and ill, carrying their fight.

If when I go, memory sparks a precious tender thought ... Wherein one recalls that I raised my hand and also fought.

So, if a home is happier 'cause I was there and tried ... Then, friend, not only did I live—I never really died.

– Sean Yeedell

☙

Jonathan then said to him (David), "Tomorrow is the new moon; and you will be missed, since your place will be empty."[11]

☙

The length of life has no bearing on the meaning of life. It is not the quantity of years that one accumulates which is of primary importance but the kind of life one leads—the individual can reach a ripe old age without any significant meaning to his life, just as it is possible to find purpose in a relatively short span of years. The task, then, is to multiply achievements rather than years. For when man seeks only years, he is nothing more than a human adding machine. His ultimate contribution is a distinction no greater than that enjoyed by a grain of sand on a desert. If life is meaningful, then quantity is not important. The real tragedy of death occurs when men are more concerned with how long they may live rather than with how they may live. The real tragedy is not when a task is left unfinished by a worker who is called away, but when the task is never begun at all. The two least important statistics of a man's life are placed upon his tombstone—when he was born and when he died. It is not the length of one's life—rather it is the breadth of his sympathies for others; it is the depth of his understanding of life's meaning; it is the height of his aspirations that are important.

– Earl Grollman[12]

11. 1 Samuel 20:18
12. *Explaining Death to Children*

They are not dead
Whose words of kindness said
Ever quicken hearts that beat
And still direct the upward course
Of lives that yearn and seek.
They are not gone
Whose deeds of bounty done
Bestow their blessings now
And on those yet to come.
They are not o'er
Whose bosoms bore new life.
Whose breath made other souls to breath
And kindled loves that never leave. Earth cannot hold
What minds unfold
The book may pass away
But not the story that is told.
The love that was our treasured one
Is something that is never done;
It lights our paths
We, too, in turn,
Shall let it kindly radiance glow
For lives the future is to know.
For every life that each one knows
Is but a bud, whose beauty grows
From on that single stem of life;
And all its shades of joy in store
Are hues bestowed by lives before.
He who beholds life's unity
Must then affirm, "There is no death
For every life that beauty sought
Can never more return to nought
One lived, that it can ne'er expire
Its soul has touched the life entire."

– Author and source unknown

Do Not Stand at My Grave and Weep

Do not stand at my grave and weep.
I am not there. I do not sleep.
I am a thousand winds that blow.
I am a diamond glint of snow.
I am the sunlight on ripened grain.
I am the gentle autumn rain.
When you awake in the morning hush,
I am the swift, uplifting rush
of quiet birds in circling flight.
I am the soft star shine at night.
Do not stand by my grave and cry.
I am not there . . . I did not die.

– Mary Elizabeth Frye

Do Not Weep For Me!

Do not weep for me though I am gone.
I was, I am, I will be—
I am a beautiful memory that stirs the heart
to love and remembrance of things that were.
I will be the life-giving rain and
the gentle earth that nurtures and supports life anew.
I was a person of gentle and caring and loving ways
I am at peace, I want nothing, and
I will be with you always.
Do not weep, for my life was one of wonder and joy.
I depart in all but memory.
Remembrance is truly God's gift to those I love.
Remember me but do not weep, for I am happy.
Live life, enjoy God's gift to human kind.

It is truly wonderful.
Do not waste it.
I will be with you always in heart and mind.

> – Author Unknown

❧

Hold on to What is Good

Hold on to what is good
Even if it is a handful of earth.
Hold on to what you believe
Even if it is a tree that stands by itself.
Hold on to what you must do
Even if it is a long way from here.
Hold on to life
Even it is easier to let go.
Hold onto my hand
Even if I have gone away from you.

> – Nancy C. Wood

❧

A mountain keeps an echo deep inside. That's how I hold your voice.

> – Rumi

❧

For he hath torn, and he will heal us,
He hath smitten, and He will bind us up.[13]

❧

---

13. *Tanakh*, Hosea 6:1

Prayer at the Funeral of Someone Who Died by Suicide

Let there be no whispering, no secrets here:
Our hearts are broken.
[Name] took his/her own life.
And even though it might appear
that s/he died by his/her own hand,
no one does this without great, coercing pain,
inner suffering that seems to have no end,
even though we wish
s/he knew that no agony is forever.
Source of compassion, help us to cry out loud,
to hold each other gently,
to live with unanswerable questions,
normal feelings of anger and guilt,
and this gaping hole of loss.
Help us to reach out to others who are suffering,
to show them our love, to say the kind word,
and that this is not a choice we condone
or is worth imitation.
It is hard to see the divine image in the lives of those who suffer.
The sun sets and rises.
We put one foot in front of the other.
We hold our hearts in our hands.
We lift them up to You, God of eternal peace,
and to each other.
Help us live each day.
Amen.

– Joseph Meszler[14]

❧

14. *Witnesses to the One*

A Prayer for Those Left Behind After the Suicide of a Loved One

May the One who blessed our ancestors, Abraham, Isaac, Jacob, Sarah, Rebecca, Rachel and Leah and all those who came after them, bless those of us living in the shadow of the valley of death, left behind because of the suffering of a dear soul who took their own life.

May our connection with the One who is the Source of All Blessing, continually remind us that our memories of our loved ones are for a blessing. *Zichronam livracha.* May we be able to look at their life and not only their suffering and death. May we learn to understand in time that memories of their life bless our days. May we know through our memories of their life, they too, are blessed wherever they rest. May they be protected by the God of Compassion.

When the memories of their life's suffering come to us, give us the strength and courage to feel compassion and love for them. Help us feel the companionship of families, friends, ancestors and the Divine Presence to protect and nourish us in times of distress. May we find the healing possible through sharing our whole experience with others, including feelings of regret and shame, relief and anger, grief and sorrow, unanswered questions, and deep love.

Source of All Life, surround us with grace and spread over us a *sukkat shalom*, a shelter of peace and wholeness. And let us say Amen.

– Rabbi Chaya Gusfield

Prayer for Those Who Have Died By Suicide

Bless, O God of eternal life,
all who have died
by their own hand.
Grant them peace
from their inner turmoil
and the compassion of your love.
Comfort those who mourn

their loved ones.

Strengthen them to face the questions and pain,

the guilt and anger,

the irreparable loss.

Help us to reach out in love

to others who prefer death

to the choices of life

tend to their families who grieve.

Amen.

– Rev. Dr. Vienna Cobb Anderson

Bibliography

Brenneman, Ellen. "For a Younger Person" in *First Tears over the Loss of Your Child* by Linda Anderson. Skokie, IL: Acta Publications, 2009, p. 84. Used with permission.

Campbell, Frank R., Ph.D., LCSW, C.T in his unpublished manuscript "The Canyon of Why: Metaphors for Healing from Sudden and Traumatic Loss."

Cobb Anderson, Vienna. "Prayer For Those Who Have Committed Suicide." Beliefnet. http.//www.beliefnet.com/Prayers/Christian/Death/Prayer-For-Those-Who-Have-Committed-Suicide.aspx. (permission granted)

Corona, Vicki. *Tahitian Choreographies: Intermediate to Advanced Level Female Instruction.* Earth Dance International Publishing. http://www.amazon.com/Tahitian-Choreographies-Vicki-Corona/dp/1585130087/ref=sr_1_4?s=books&ie=UTF8&qid=1461716576&sr=1-4&keywords=vicki+corona+tahitian

Downing, Frederick L. *Elie Wiesel: A Religious Biography.* Mason, GA: Mercer University Press, 2008.

Fitzgerald, William John. *Words of Comfort: What to Say at times of Sadness or Loss.* Phoenix, AZ: Tau, 1999.

Frye, Mary Elizabeth. "Do Not Stand At My Grave And Weep—1932" Poemhunter.com. http://www.poemhunter.com/poem/do-not-stand-at-my-grave-and-weep/.

Grollman, Earl. *Explaining Death to Children.* Boston, MA: Beacon, 1967.

Hatch, Edwin. "Toward Fields of Light." in *A Jewish Service During Shiva.* AJP (Association for Progressive Judaism) 2014, p. 20

Levine, Amy-Jill. *The Misunderstood Jew: The Church and the Scandal of the Jewish Jesus.* San Francisco, CA: HarperSanFrancisco, 2006.

Meszler, Joseph. *Witnesses to the One: The Spiritual History of the Sh'ma.* Woodstock, VT: Jewish Lights, a Division of Longhill Partners, Inc., 2006. Originally printed in the Huffing Post Religion Blog, July 22, 2013. Permission granted.

Rumi, Jalaluddin. "Quotable Quote." *Good Reads.* http://www.goodreads.com/quotes/52544-a-mountain-keeps-an-echo-deep-inside-that-s-how-i

Scolnic, Benjamin Edidin. "Midrash, PC, and Eve." Midstream 38, no. 6 (August/September 1992): 32–33.

Tanakh: The Holy Scriptures. Philadelphia: Jewish Publication Society, 1917.

The United Methodist Book of Worship. Nashville, TN. United Methodist Publishing House, 1992. (Permission granted)

Weedn, Flavia. *Flavia and the Dream Maker.* San Rafael, CA: Cedco, 1999.

Wood, Nancy C. "Hold on to What is Good." *National Alliance on Mental Illness, Utah.* © 1974 Nancy C. Wood, reprinted from *Many Winters*, courtesy of the Nancy Wood Literary Trust

Chapter Seven

Giving Voice to Pain
Using Psalms of Lament to Address Suicide Grief

Terry L. Smith, Ed.D.

[This chapter represents a type of counseling and comfort that no social worker or psychologist can do with the bereaved.—Ed.]

The experience of profound loss can tax one's physical, emotional, and spiritual resources and one's ability to cope. Models of grief counseling share a common denominator: one must accept the reality of the loss and experience the pain associated with the loss.[1]

This is particularly true when the experience of loss involves suicide. Jordan says that compared to other losses, those bereaved by suicide experience higher levels of social alienation and stigmatization.[2] This is further complicated by the difficulty in making sense of the act which has served as a "powerful rupturing of the mourner's assumptive world."[3] So much of one's understanding of how the world operates is disrupted when a loved one takes his or her own life.

---

1. Worden in *Death, Dying and Bereavement*, 91–104.
2. Jordan in *Death, Dying, and Bereavement.*
3. Ibid., 350.

Jordan also identifies the complex "tasks of healing"[4] that are relevant for most survivors, including containment of the trauma, dosing the grief, developing a compassionate narrative, managing social incompetence, transforming the bond with the deceased, memorializing the deceased, and learning to find meaning and purpose in a changed world.

Scarry acknowledges the difficulty in giving language to pain, that pain is language shattering and thus makes it challenging to share our experience in words.[5] Similarly, Wiesel suggests that certain experiences—he notes abuse and torture—drive speech to silence so that it is easier to suppress the memory of such events or gag them in silence than to bring them to memory and speech with all the pain this entails.[6] Jinkins insists that sufferers need an honest language that allows them to vocalize their sense of loss and uncertainty, their fears of what the future will hold, and their worries about how to deal with the changes in their lives.[7] Cook calls this "ungagging the voice of the victim."[8]

Giving voice and language to suffering is precisely what happens in the Biblical laments, most notably the psalms of lament.[9] Though not responding specifically to suffering caused by a suicide, these laments give shape to and supply words to rail about all that is unbearable. They hold up to the sufferer a poetic mirror of their own spiritual, mental, and emotional struggles, their despair and their shattered confidence. The fact that lament psalms are the most common type suggests that lament was voiced regularly.[10] Billman and Migliore describe lament as "the language of the painful incongruity between lived experience and the promises of God."[11] It is clear that profound pain demands a response. This essay explores the value of lament psalms in understanding and addressing a mind-staggering event such as suicide.

Psalms of lament (notably 13, 22, 38, 41–42, 55, 56, 60, 69, 73, 77, 80, and 88) arise from times of trouble and express the fullness of human suffering with radical honesty. Brueggemann argues that these psalms are

4. Ibid., 355.

5. Scarry, *The Body in Pain*.

6. Billman and Migliore, *Rachel's Cry*.

7. Jinkins, *In the House of the Lord*.

8. Cook, *The Living Pulpit*, 4–5.

9. Brown and Miller, *Lamen.t*

10. Webster and Beach, *The Place of Lament in Christian Life*, 387–402.

11. Billman and Migliore, *Rachel's Cry*, 103.

a form of complaint that insists that things are not right in the present arrangement, and the speaker, considering the situation to be intolerable, insists that it is God's obligation to change things. The main point, Brueggemann says, is that life is not right nor what it was promised to be.[12] Those bereaved by suicide would definitely agree.

Psalms of lament can be used by the grief-stricken as their own prayers to give a voice to horrors and pain. The psalms invite readers to look in to their own doubt, anger, despair, and broken faith.[13] Going further, Lee (2010) encourages those who grieve to create lament lyrics, that is, use their own words and experiences to create poetry, much like the psalmist did, that allows one to transform their pain into empowerment.[14] In view of the language shattering nature of grief, Niemeyer said that literary and narrative methods can help people express complex experiences as well as to integrate them into the new normal that they are seeking to establish. He observed, "Often the richly figurative speech afforded by poetry permits the bereaved to transcend the limits of literal language and give voice to intimate personal meanings and promote their evolution in ways that sometimes surprise the poets themselves."[15]

Schirmer found the lament psalms to have a cathartic value as he struggled with his own grief. In the worst times he paradoxically found comfort in Psalm 44:19. He observed, "These words, and the words of many of the lament psalms, have been cathartic in that they have encouraged me to utter my cry and have provided the words to express it."[16]

Another value of the lament psalms is that they validate and normalize the sadness, hurt, alienation, questions, doubts, anger, confusion, and bewilderment that accompany the grief process. By connecting with the deepest levels of despair the pain is legitimized, experienced, and released. Cook observed that one can no longer believe the victim to be subhuman after hearing his or her personal, human cry of lament and, after witnessing their pain, can come to empathize.[17] Rather than seeking or offering a palliative or superficial reassurance so common in our culture, pain is transformed through the power of connection in suffering. Importantly,

12. Brueggemann, *Journal for the Study of the Old Testament*, 57–71.

13. Cook, *The Living Pulpit*, 4–5.

14. Lee, *Lyrics of Lament*

15. Niemeyer, *Grief Matters*, 65.

16. Schirmer, *Lutheran Theological Journal*, 33–35.

17. Cook, *The Living Pulpit*, 4–5.

because the specific circumstances of the psalms are not identified, they may be applied to all types of loss, including suicide.

The lament psalms can reduce the sense of isolation that those bereaved by suicide might feel as they realize that they are in concert with a long line of sufferers. Others before them have asked, *how long, O Lord, how long,* or *why do you hide your face from me* or observed that *Darkness is my closest companion.* In isolation, the power of pain grows more ominous and hurtful. Flesher noted that in ancient Israel, lamentation was often a community event.[18] Family and friends of the grief-laden individual were expected to show support by participating in the rituals of lament with the mourner. Job's three friends sit with him in silence for seven days to empathize with his deep grief. To show solidarity in such a situation was to powerfully declare themselves as covenantal partners with Job.[19]

Mackey adds that lament was ritualistic in the Hebraic experience.[20] Entire companies of the faithful would join the expressions of mourning when it appeared God was silent in a particular circumstance. Regrettably, the prayer of lament is noticeably absent in the church. Meyer found that psalms of lament are poorly represented in the worship books of most mainline denominations.[21] Too often, it seems the Church is in collusion with the culture's tendency to ignore the experience of loss in hopes that it will ultimately go away on its own. Wolterstorff acknowledged that lament does not market well in our churches.[22]

The psalms of lament provide structure for the process of grief itself. Brueggemann[23] and Capps[24] say that the *form* of the lament facilitated grieving and made possible the subsequent transformation. Brueggemann says that the central movement of the lament is a "sharp, discontinued step from pleas to praise, from brokenness to wholeness."[25] The form serves the function of rehabilitation. Specifically, the typical lament begins with a cry for help and a description of the distress, moves to an appeal to God and

---

18. Flesher, *The Living Pulpit,* 36–37.

19. Job 2:12–13.

20. Mackey, The Living Pulpit, 48.

21. Meyer, *Lutheran Quarterly,* 67–78.

22. Wolterstorff, *Calvin Theological* Journal, 42–52.

23. Bruggemann, *Journal for the Study of the Old Testament,* 57–71.

24. Capps, *Lament,* 70–79

25. Bruggemann, *Journal for the Study of the Old Testament,* 57–71.

provides reasons for divine intervention, and ends on a note of praise. The lament psalms are structured to move from sorrow to joy.

Capps says that one reason the personal lament form has survived for so long is that the originals did not specify the conditions that gave rise to it.[26] Thus, the lament can be adapted to fit the new circumstances of the contemporary griever. The range of emotions represented in the lament psalms permits the sufferer to enter the process at any point and to find that in the words of the ancients he or she may recognize his or her own experience.

Anne Weems, author of poetry, stories, and meditations, lost her son an hour after his twenty-first birthday. While she was still absorbed by her grief, Walter Brueggemann compassionately directed her attention to the lament psalms and suggested she compose her own. In her resultant book, *Psalms of Lament*, her prayers model the power of expressing oneself in this way and are honest, poignant cries of pain and faith.

The psalms of lament invite one to listen to anguish without judgment or the need to superficially reassure. Wolterstorff described the anguished questions of those who grieve and for the need for others to listen.[27] He observed, "If you think your task as comforter is to tell me that really, all things considered, it's not so bad, you do not sit with me in my grief but place yourself off in the distance away from me. Over there, you are of no help. What I need to hear from you is that you are with me in my desperation. To comfort me, you have to come close. Come sit beside me on my mourning bench."[28]

Reading and contemplating the lament psalms can attune one's ears to hear the anger, despair, loneliness, or terror of others. Such study prepares one to be what Wolfelt refers to as "companioning" the bereaved.[29] Suderman said that, as one raises his or her voice to God in a personal lament, they also invite the social audience to hear the pained cries, solicit their empathy, and incite them to become more active in addressing the predicament felt, in this case, by the survivor.[30] Brueggemann notes that the "words of lament move the petitioner from voiceless victim to speaking agent, thereby challenging listeners to also move from a passive to active stance."[31]

26. Capps, *Lament*, 70–79

27. Wolterstorff, *Lament for a Son*.

28. Wolterstorff, *Lament for a Son*, 34.

29. Wolfelt, *Companioning the Bereaved*.

30. Suderman, *Journal of Theological Interpretation*, 201–218.

31. Brueggemann, *Interpretation*, 263–275.

The psalms of lament give a voice of hope in the midst of despair. Balentine said that lamentation is a "journey towards God, not a final destination."[32] Brown and Miller assert that lament is first of all a form of prayer. It arises "out of the reality of human existence; it assumes that there is something beyond that reality that can transform human existence without destroying it."[33] Black goes even further and says that the "spine of lament is hope." He said this is not an empty optimism that "things will get better" but is a deep and irrepressible conviction that deliverance is at hand.[34] Margalit is reminded of the Jewish *Kaddish*, the "mourner's prayer," which is praise offered in the future tense. The mourner is not asked to praise God in this moment when the grief is so intense but to affirm that God will bless the future.[35] Thus, the laments teach spiritual survival. They do not sink into permanent despair but grasp toward recovery. They model how one might continue to embrace hope and come back after disaster. This is what O'Connor calls "lamenting back to life."[36]

Jordan and associates acknowledged that those who are grieving the loss of a significant person to suicide have begun to speak up and insist on acceptance, support, and action from their communities. The authors assert that suicide must become an acceptable topic for discussion in all of our social institutions, whether it be in the media, schools, or certainly in churches, synagogues, temples, and mosques. Suicide must stop being the "unspeakable event." Otherwise, the concerted efforts of survivors to learn to articulate their pain in the first place could be stifled. Survivors must not be stigmatized but recognized as people grieving after the death of a loved one due to complex factors we can only begin to imagine.[37] This chapter has sought to explore one way that survivors can embrace the words of sufferers from a previous generation, use them to articulate their pain, and began the process of reconciling themselves to such losses. Maybe, too, the lament psalms can more fully equip those who seek to companion the survivors on their loss journey.

32. Balentine, *Journal for Preachers*, 12–17.

33. Brown and Miller, *Lament*.

34. Black, *Lament*, 47–58.

35. Margalit, *The Living Pulpit*, 16–18.

36. O'Connor, *Interpretation*, 34–47.

37. Jordan, et al, *Grief After Suicide*.

Bibliography

Balentine, Samuel. "Preaching the Prayers of the Old Testament." *Journal for Preachers* 17 (2004) 12–17.

Billman, Kathleen D. and Daniel L. Migliore. *Rachel's Cry: Prayer of Lament and Rebirth of Hope*. Cleveland, OH: United Church Press, 1999.

Black, Clifton. "The Persistence of the Wounds." In *Lament: Reclaiming Practices in Pulpit, Pew, and Public Square*, Sally Brown and Patrick Miller, eds. Louisville, KY: Westminster/John Knox Press, 2005, 47–58.

Brown, Sally A. and Patrick D. Miller, eds. *Lament: Reclaiming Practices in Pulpit, Pew, and Public Square*. Louisville, KY: Westminster/John Knox Press, 2005.

Brueggemann, Walter. "The Costly Loss of Lament." In *Journal for the Study of the Old Testament* 36 (1977) 57–71.

———. "The Formfulness of Loss." *Interpretation* 31 (1986): 263–275.

Capps, Donald. "Nervous Laughter: Lament, Death Anxiety, and Humor." In *Lament: Reclaiming Practices in Pulpit, Pew, and Public Square*. Sally A. Brown and Patrick D. Miller, eds. Louisville, KY: Westminster/John Knox Press, 2005. 70–79.

Cook, Stephen L. "Lamentation, Praise, and Collective Violence." *The Living Pulpit* 11 (2002) 4–5.

Flesher, LeAnn Snow. "Lamentation and the Canonical Psalms." *The Living Pulpit* 11 (2002) 36–37.

Jinkins, Michael. *In the House of the Lord: Inhabiting the Psalms of Lament*. Collegeville, MN: Liturgical Press, 1998.

Jordan, John. "Grief After Suicide: The Evolution of Suicide Postvention." In *Death, Dying, and Bereavement: Contemporary Perspectives, Institutions, and Practices*. J. Stillion and Thomas Attig, eds. New York: Springer, 2015.

———, John L. McIntosh, Iris M. Bolton, Frank K. Campbell, Joanne L. Harpel, and Michelle Linn-Gust. "A Call to Action: Building Clinical and Programmatic Support for Suicide Survivors." In *Grief After Suicide: Understanding the Consequences and Caring for the Survivors*. John Jordan and John McIntosh, eds. New York and London: Routledge Taylor & Francis Group, 2011.

Lee, Nancy C. *Lyrics of Lament: From Tragedy to Transformation*. Minneapolis, MN: Fortress Press, 2010.

Mackey, Jeffrey. "The Emotion of Biblical Song: A Reflection on Lament and Praise." *The Living Pulpit* 11 (2002) 48.

Margalit, Nathan. "The Great, the Mighty, and the Awesome: Lamentation and Praise in the Talmud." *The Living Pulpit* 11 (2002) 16–18.

Meyer, Lester. "A Lack of Laments in the Church's Use of the Psalter." *Lutheran Quarterly* (1993) 67–78.

Niemeyer, Robert. "Meaning Making in the Midst of Loss." *Grief Matters* 9 (2009) 62–65.

O'Connor, Kathleen. "Lamenting Back to Life." *Interpretation* 62 (2008) 34–47.

Scarry, Elaine. *The Body in Pain: The Making and Unmaking of the World*. New York: Oxford University Press, 1985.

Schirmer, Geoffrey F. "Lamenting in Christ: A Personal Spiritual Account." *Lutheran Theological Journal* 35 (2001) 33–35.

Suderman, W. Derek. "The Cost of Losing Lament for the Community of Faith: On Brueggemann, Ecclesiology, and the Social Audience of Prayer." *Journal of Theological Interpretation* 6 (2012) 201–218.

Utley, Don, "The Gift of Lament." *Leaven* (1996) 21–22.

Webster, Brian and David Beach. "The Place of Lament in the Christian Life." *Bibliotheca Sacra*, 164 (2007) 387–402.

Wolterstorff, Nicholas. *Lament for a Son*. Grand Rapids, MI: William B. Eerdmans, 1987.

———. "If God is Good and Sovereign, Why Lament?" *Calvin Theological* Journal, 64 (2001) 42–52.

Weems, Anne. *Psalms of Lament*. Louisville: Westminster/John Knox Press, 1995.

Wolfelt, Alan. *Companioning the Bereaved: A soulful guide for caregivers*. Fort Collins: Companion, 2006.

Worden, J. William. "Theoretical Perspective on Loss and Grief." In *Death, Dying and Bereavement: Contemporary Perspectives, Institutions, and Practices*. Judith M. Stillion and Thomas Attig, eds. New York: Springer, 2015.

Chapter Eight

Postvention
Clergy Self-Care in the Wake of Suicide

MELINDA MOORE, PHD, AND RABBI DANIEL ROBERTS, DD,
DMIN, FT

> The man who articulates the movements of his inner life, who can
> give names to his varied experiences, need no longer be a victim of
> himself, but is able slowly and consistently to remove the obstacles
> that prevent the spirit from entering. He is able to create space for
> Him whose heart is greater than his, whose eyes see more than his,
> and whose hands can heal more than his.[1]

Our Experiences With Suicide

In a legend recorded in the Talmud (ancient Jewish literature), the
prophet Elijah is asked, "When will the Messiah come?"
    Elijah replied, "Go and ask him yourself."
    "Where is he?" the man replied excitedly.
    "Sitting at the gates of the city," replied Elijah.
    "How shall I know him?" quizzed the man.
    Slowly, Elijah responds: "He is sitting among the poor, covered
with wounds. Whereas the other healers unbind all the wounded
at the same time and then bind them up again, he unbinds one

---

1. Nouwen, *The Wounded Healer*, 38

at a time and binds it up again, saying to himself, 'Perhaps I shall be needed; if so, I must always be ready so as not to delay for a moment.'"[2]

From this story, we learn that the Messiah, too, is covered with wounds, allowing the other wounded to heal all their wounds at one time, while he sits and cares for each individual wound in case he is needed. Modern clergy may find this image familiar. We heal others' wounds wholly and completely to the best of our ability but we rarely look at our individual injuries with any kind of introspection. We always worry that we will be needed by another, or we are too proud to acknowledge that we, too, can be wounded.

We are called upon infrequently to officiate at a funeral of suicide or to counsel someone who is suicidal. Yet this we know, as authors of this book, *such an experience is totally unlike the "normal" losses through natural death, accident, divorce, or illnesses.* While the latter take their tolls upon our ministry, in terms of psychological stress, they are nothing like the anxiety and questioning when one officiates at the funeral of someone who died by suicide. In *The Wounded Healer: Ministry in Contemporary Society,* Henri Nouwen draws out the beautiful paradox of the fruits of our own injuries as instruments of healing for the people we serve. *In our own woundedness, we can become a source of life to others.* The gifts of understanding, acceptance, and communion with someone who truly understands are resplendent, if we open ourselves up to self-reflection and awareness.

This is best demonstrated in Thornton Wilder's one act play, "The Angel That Troubled the Waters," based on John 5:1–4.[3] The pool of Bethesda had the power to heal whenever an angel stirred its waters. One day, a physician comes to the pool early in the morning hoping to be the first in line and longing to be healed of his melancholy. An angel appears but blocks the physician just as he is ready to step into the water. The angel tells the physician to draw back, for this moment is not for him. The physician pleads for help in a broken voice, but the angel insists that healing is not intended for him. The angel proclaims, "Without your wounds, where would your power be? It is your melancholy that makes your low voice tremble into the hearts of men and women. The very angels themselves cannot persuade the wretched and blundering children on earth as can one human being broken

---

2. Schram, *Tales of Elijah the Prophet*, xxviii

3. Wilder, *Collected Short Plays Vol. 2*, 71–76

on the wheels of living. In Love's service, only wounded soldiers can serve. Physician, draw back."

Later, the man who enters the pool first and is healed rejoices in his good fortune and, turning to the physician, says, "Please come with me. It is only an hour to my home. My son is lost in dark thoughts. I do not understand him and only you have ever lifted his mood. There is also my daughter: since her child died, she sits in the shadow. She will not listen to us but she will listen to you."[4]

As clergy we are in positions of authority and leadership, people turn to us looking for models of dealing with suicide. How we respond to an individual who is suffering or how we conduct a service may influence or predict people's thoughts or behavior as they experience grief.

In the journey of conducting a suicide funeral, when helping the survivors to reconcile the loss or counselling someone dealing with depression, we may be scarred and wounded psychologically and emotionally. Most people, blessedly, have had no experience with suicide; the *unwounded* have no concept of that pain and anguish. To more effectively serve those who seek us out for comfort, support, and guidance, we must explore our beliefs and attitudes about suicide. Delve into the subject theologically and secularly. Consider how your viewpoints may aid or hinder our service to bereaved. Just as important to your spiritual and psychological health, think about how your beliefs might delay your own recuperation.

Self-Care in the Wake of Suicide

For clinicians who have lost a client to suicide, an online community of support has emerged at the American Association of Suicidology's Clinician-Survivor Task Force website. There is an abundance of resources for clinicians, as well as a listserve that allows clinicians from around the globe to connect and support each other. This confidential message board unites people who either are experiencing the suicide of a client or managing personal experiences of suicide. It is extremely helpful in addressing the sense of guilt or failure to act in a timely manner. At the writing of this book, there is a plan in the works at the American Association of Suicidology to develop a similar resource for clergy. Please check the website listed in the Resources for that forthcoming Clergy-Survivor Task Force website.

4. "The Wounded Healer, Part 2"

Don't go the journey alone! We cannot encourage you enough as clergy to seek out a close friend, colleague, or trusted advisor with whom to share your spiritual and psychological dilemmas. Just as clinicians often find it necessary to engage in consultation teams or peer supervision groups, clergy will find it helpful to reach out for support when confronted with a suicide or when ministering to a congregant who is suicidal.

What to Do When a Congregant or a Family Member of a Parishioner Dies by Suicide

In ministering to your congregants, it is important to have established relationships with mental health professionals experienced in caring for the suicide bereaved. Collect information on Survivors of Suicide Support groups in your community by investigating what groups are available through the American Association of Suicidology's Survivors Of Suicide group list or online resources, e.g., Parents of Suicide Online Support, Alliance of Hope. Often, hospice organizations will have access to well-trained counselors that can be called upon for support. Funeral homes may offer bereavement support groups. Additionally, the Compassionate Friends is dedicated to parents who have lost a child to any cause of death.

If you were suicide exposed (witnessed a suicide or had someone you know die by suicide) or are bereaved by suicide (had someone close to you die by suicide), self-care is vital. Seek support in your faith community. Find a counselor or a spiritual guide who is competent to speak to the unique grief that suicide imparts. Feelings of guilt often hinder seeking self-care in the wake of a congregant's suicide. Guilt is a natural emotion as a consequence of suicide, as are shame, isolation, embarrassment, fear, depression, and the subthreshold symptoms of Post-Traumatic Stress Disorder. Consulting with a professional may help you determine if you are experiencing any of these symptoms.

We remind you that you have been through an existential crisis. Placed before you is the awareness that you, too, can choose between life and death. Although you choose life, life's twin may call when things are difficult and dark. Consider joining a local suicide support group yourself, if necessary. Don't be too proud. You, too, are a wounded healer.

Taking Time Out and Taking Care of Yourself

You deserve to take time off to nurse your wounds. Just as with illness or surgery, you need time to recuperate, so it is as a wounded healer. It is easy to fall into the trap of feeling guilty when taking time away from your ministry to care for yourself. However, this will rejuvenate you and make you a more effective pastor. You deserve time to rejoice with your family. You deserve time to work out, take a walk, play a sport you enjoy, go to the theater or out with friends. You need to engage in whatever spiritual practice inspires you. Flip through your prayer book until you find a prayer that touches your soul. In the darkened sanctuary, give thanks to God for the talent and sensitivity to save a life or help the bereaved face and reconcile the loss. We need to stop and praise God that we were elected to be one of God's instruments in building the universe.

Resources of Support

Alliance of Hope: http://www.allianceofhope.org/
American Association of Suicidology Clinician-Survivor Task Force: http://mypage.iu.edu/~jmcintos/therapists_mainpg.htm
American Association of Suicidology Survivor of Suicide Support Groups: http://www.suicidology.org/suicide-survivors/sos-directory
International Center for Women's Ministries: http://www.centerforwomensministries.org/
Parents of Suicides and Friends and Family of Suicides Online Support: http://www.pos-ffos.com/

Bibliography

Nouwen, Henri J. M. *The Wounded Healer: Ministry in Contemporary Society*. New York: Image Books Doubleday, 1972.
Schram, Peninah. *Tales of Elijah the Prophet*. New York: Jason Aronson, 1991.
Wilder, Thornton. *The Collected Short Plays of Thornton Wilder Volume 2*. Edited by Donald Gallup and A. Tappan. Wilder. New York: Theatre Communications Group, 1997.
"The Wounded Healer, Part 2." International Center For Women's Ministries. September 6, 2011. Accessed August 5, 2016. http://www.centerforwomensministries.org/the-wounded-healter-part-2/.

Chapter Nine

Suicide and Spirituality
A Case Study of Therapeutic Alliance

Kenneth J. Doka, Ph.D.

Introduction

Historically, the Judeo-Christian tradition has been inimical to suicide. This tradition arose, in part, from Judaism's emphasis on the sanctity of life, the belief that life came from God and could only be taken by God. As the earliest Christian missionaries, themselves converts from Judaism, encountered a Roman culture that did not share that belief in the sanctity of life—and, in fact, encouraged suicide in many conditions[1]—the missionaries offered strong condemnation. In addition, the early Christian fathers faced other dilemmas during periods of persecution. While extolling the sacrifice of martyrdom, these early Church leaders also had to warn followers from actively seeking it.

Over the years, condemnation of suicide grew stronger, particularly within Christendom. Persons who died from suicide were denied Christian funerals and refused burial within sanctified ground. In theology, they were viewed as mortally sinned by that very act and consigned to eternal damnation. In the early twentieth century, as the field of psychology developed, most mainline Christian denominations softened their stance. While still

---

1. In Rome, the welfare of the family transcended the individual. In Roman law, the state could confiscate wealth and property after a guilty verdict or a variety of crimes. Hence, the judge's decision to suspend sentencing for a few days was a clear message to defendant to take his or her own life before a judgment and sentence was pronounced.

condemning the act of suicide, most churches now consider attempting or dying by suicide to be a symptom rather than a sin. Most now offer compassion rather than condemnation. Yet, in more fundamentalist denominations, the early opprobrium remains.

Case Description

Tim, a fifty-four-year-old man, belongs to a fundamentalist church that shares the traditional view of suicide. His oldest son, Mark, who lived with Tim and his wife, Emily, recently died by suicide at age twenty-four. Throughout his life, Mark struggled with substance abuse and mental illness.

At the urging of his wife, Tim has sought counseling to deal with Mark's suicide. Many of his feelings and issues are common to parents experiencing a child's suicide. He feels guilt over the death, questioning his parenting, regretting arguments with Mark, and second-guessing his decisions regarding Mark's myriad problems. Tim obsessively reviews Mark's last days, trying to see if he missed clues that could have allowed him to intervene and prevent his death. He has intense anger toward his son, both for his way of life and the manner of his death.

These issues are complicated by Tim's faith system. Tim wonders if he was as a good a Christian father as he aspired to be and feels guilty that he could not infuse Mark with good Christian values and a strong faith. Tim is furthermore deeply concerned and convinced that, as result of his suicide, Mark is condemned to spend eternity in Hell. Sadly, this belief is supported by his pastor and spiritual advisor who, preaching at the funeral, admonished the mourners not to "follow Mark in the fiery journey to eternal damnation."

Problem

Tim is deeply struggling with Mark's suicide and has both psychological and spiritual complications in his grief.

Analysis

Suicide by its very nature often generates problematic grief reactions. Jordan and McIntosh describe some of the particular aspects of grief after suicide.[2] They note, for example, clinical accounts that emphasize, among other reactions, guilt, anger, shame and stigma, relief, and a search for meaning. Tim is certainly struggling with many of those problems. His anger and guilt have already been described, yet he also feels a sense of relief. Mark was difficult to live with, as Tim and Emily frequently dealt with his mood swings, legal issues (including arrests for drunk driving and drug possession), conflicts, and Tim's fears of Mark's influence on his three younger siblings. Mark's death has paradoxically led to what Tim has described as a "normal family life"—yet he also feels guilty that he experiences such relief.

Tim's search for meaning and his sense of shame and stigma are complicated by his spiritual beliefs. Tim takes fatherhood very seriously as a gift from God and a sacred calling. He wonders how he failed, at least as Mark is concerned, even as he takes pleasure in his relationship with and the achievements of his younger children. He wonders if Mark was somehow *possessed* by a malign spirit—again, a belief suggested by his pastor. Yet, even that is not comforting. *How could God allow that? What does that say of Tim's own parenting?* Tim's shame is intense. It is as if Mark's death is a deep and public blemish on his own role as a Christian and a parent. He is deeply troubled that, because of these failures, his son is now consigned to Hell.

Counseling Goal

To assist Tim in coping with his son's death by suicide and grief complicated by his spiritual beliefs.

Intervention

It becomes clear that Tim will make little progress in counseling as long as he believes his son is eternally damned. While the counselor shares a Christian faith with Tim, his own denomination holds very different views on suicide. The counselor's spirituality has little in common with Tim's, and his queries about his faith lack credibility.

2. Jordan and McIntosh, *Grief after suicide*

As an adjunct to therapy, the counselor refers Tim to Pastor John, a graduate student who is ordained in Tim's denomination. They begin a Bible study together about the Israelite judge Samson, a man known for his strength but struggling with self-destructive tendencies. Samson falls in love with a Philistine (Israel's enemy at the time), Delilah, who entreats Samson to tell her his source of strength. He responds with lies. For example, Samson tells Delilah that if he is tied with seven thongs, he will be powerless. He awakens surrounded by Philistines only to snap off the ropes and scare off his attackers. Eventually, Samson tells Delilah the truth. Unsurprisingly to everyone but Samson, he is captured. Blinded and tortured, he is taken to the main Philistine temple to be publicly mocked. There, Samson asks God for one more feat of strength. His wish granted, Samson takes down the temple, killing himself and his enemies. Pastor John stressed Samson's self-destructive nature, yet pointed out that in Hebrews 11, Samson is noted to be saved. As they discussed the story, Tim became convinced of God's mercy.

The counselor and Tim, now unburdened by fear, were able to explore his grief over the death of his son. Therapy took a traditional turn, utilizing modalities such as the internalized other. Developed by Nancy Moules, this is a variation of the empty chair technique.[3] Here, Tim spoke to an empty chair as if it were his son, Mark, then sat on the chair and answered as he believed Mark would respond. In addition, the counselor utilized therapeutic rituals,[4] such as a ritual of reconciliation, where Tim forgave his son and himself, and a ritual of transition, where he affirmed his belief in Mark's entrance to heaven.

Conclusion

Suicide can be an inherently complicating loss, especially when spiritual beliefs enhance shame and stigma and interfere with a quest for meaning and completion. Counselors need to be sensitive to such beliefs and, overall, to the role that spirituality may play in suicide bereavement. Counselors also must recognize that they may lack credibility in challenging or exploring these beliefs with their clients—particularly if they do not share that faith system. Such exploration may generate defensiveness in clients, who perceive their faith is being challenged. In such cases, it helps to develop

3. Moules, OMEGA, 187–99.
4. Doka and Martin, *Grieving beyond gender*

therapeutic alliances with local clergy/religious leaders who can assist therapy. In the case of Mark and Tim, for example, the counselor would be unlikely to use a biblically based approach or even have credibility with it. Tim benefitted from the counselor's receptiveness to work with clergy in such an alliance. Utilizing therapeutic ritual also enabled Tim to integrate his beliefs with the therapy. In fact, Pastor John participated in the Ritual of Transition, thereby adding an element of validity.

In summary, suicide can generate a spiritual crisis that may tax many counselors. In such cases, therapeutic alliances can offer opportunities for counselors, clergy, and clients to work together and, in fact, grow and learn together.

Bibliography

Doka, Kenneth J. and Terry L. Martin. *Grieving Beyond Gender: Understanding the Ways Men and Women Grieve*. New York: Routledge, Taylor, and Francis, 2010.

Jordan, John R. and John L. McIntosh, eds. *Grief After Suicide: Understanding the Consequences and Caring for the Survivors*. New York: Routledge, 2011.

Moules, Nancy J. "Internal Connections and Conversations: The Internalized Other Interview in Bereavement Work. "*OMEGA —Journal of Death and Dying* 62, no. 2 (2011) 187–99.

Chapter Ten

Now What?

Harold Ivan Smith, MA, Ed.S., FT, DMin

Throughout sacred literature, a theme flows; a leader, king, prophet dies, a crisis erupts, and the people ask, *now what?* That question has surfaced at historic moments, when FDR died in 1945, in the days following the 2000 presidential election as *counting chads* entered the political vocabulary, or in the first hours after the terrorist attack on the World Trade Center in September 2001.

Following a death by suicide, many grievers wrestle with *why?* Some are obsessed by the question and may be willing to settle for what passes for "answers." *Why* did she/he give up on life? *Why* now? *Why* this particular method?

Never be hesitant to offer hospitality to a *why* question. Worry more about suicide-grievers who are not asking *why* or are not asking the question aloud.

Grievers have taught me that even if you get an answer to a "Why?" or an anguished *"Whyyyyy!"* you do not get the deceased back. Indeed, for some, "Why?" can be an endless cul-de-sac.

Grievers have taught me that the better question is, *now what? Now what* do I do? *Now what* do we do? Clergy should encourage that question or even jumpstart the process by asking the question.

In North American culture, there seems to be a conclusion of, *we've done a funeral/memorial service/committal,* as if they were elements on a *check off* list. Indeed, some want the death ritual to be the wrap-up. There. Done!

The Indianapolis 500 motor race offers an analogy that may translate into a griever's thinking. There is, of course, the dramatic, *ladies and gentlemen, start your engines*. The infamous checked flag, however, does not wave until there has been a rolling initial lap around the track.

Tapping into your skills

Some clergy have impressive homiletical abilities; the funeral is an opportunity to *shine* as well as comfort. Other clergy have managerial skills, particularly with building programs or leading a community of faith in transition. Some clergy are fundraisers. Over the years, I have wondered at the success of clergy who do not shine in any of these categories.

I asked one church member, "Why has your minister thrived here? He cannot preach! He has no original ideas!"

Although this member agreed with my assessment, I was not prepared for his explanation.

"Yes, but when my son died, and there was nothing to be said, he kept showing up, meeting me for coffee, letting me be angry."

I am not sure where the pastor learned that technique, probably not in a school of theology. I could introduce you to others in the church who have had a similar experience. Sometimes, it was an email that said, "Thinking of you today."

There is a great hymn, "Lead On, O King Eternal," that encourages congregational singing. One day, I heard a phrase sung that I have never been able to silence in my imagination. Ernest W. Shurtleff, the hymn writer, drafted these words:

> For not with swords' loud clashing
> or roll of stirring drums
> *with deeds of love and mercy*
> *the heavenly kingdom comes.*[1]

In no seminary curriculum I have reviewed have I noticed a pastoral care class titled, "Deeds of Love and Mercy 101."

1. Ernest W. Shurtleff, "Lead On, O King Eternal" (Public Domain).

Share a copy of your eulogy with grievers

You may have spent hours writing a eulogy and may have concluded, *not bad*. The griever, however, may not have heard a word, given the depth of the pain and shock.

Make a commitment to share a copy of your eulogy with grievers *and* make yourself available to talk about your remarks or to listen to a griever's response to your effort. Yes, I understand, it is your intellectual property, but sharing the eulogy may be an invitation to further reflection and conversation.

Remember the drop off factor

I have joked that funeral homes need notaries to sit near the casket or urn. People tend to make promises in memorialization environments because they are nervous. So, when someone says, *Now, you call me if there is anything I can do*, that promise should be notarized. The griever has a coupon for an offer of help. Grievers are disappointed by the lack of follow-through.

One widow demanded, "Where are all the people who made the promises at the visitation?"

In your encounters with the grieving, you might permission a meaningful conversation by asking, "Since your loved one's suicide, who has disappointed you?" You may want to preface the question with, "People often make promises of future help but fail to follow through. Has that happened to you?" Follow up with a second question, "Since your loved one's suicide, *who has surprised you*? Has there been someone you did not think had an ounce of compassion, yet they have made themselves available to you and your family?" Another question you might ask to jumpstart conversation is, "Why do you think people have failed to come through?"

Common answers you can expect include, *people mean well but* or *people don't know what to say* or *people are too afraid of saying the wrong thing*.

Invite evaluation

In conducting celebrant services for a large funeral home, I am always evaluated for my work. Every family is asked to complete a survey that goes first to a national association and then to our management. Certainly, most families will offer some initial assessment, *thank you* or *we appreciated your sensitivity*, etc.

We need to give families more time to assess clergy contribution. It could be as simple as, *I want you to help me help the next family I serve who has experienced a suicide. What could I have said better? How could I have been more present to you? What did not help you?* It is not having judges use a one to ten scoring at the end of the ritual, but sometimes, you may have said something that veered from your original intent. Grievers may have heard something that does not reconcile with your actual words. You may have said something that distracted a griever or the audience away from the next segment of your thoughts. If you are uncomfortable conducting a service following a suicide, some element of your discomfort will come through. If you are not comfortable with conversations down the road with grievers, you miss opportunities for significant aftercare.

At the hospital where I lead grief groups, I often ask about a particular post-death concern, "Have you talked to your pastor/minister/priest/rabbi?"

Often—far too often—I hear, "Oh she's soooo busy." (No one says, "He's toooo busy!")

I want to ask, "Doing what?"

Anticipate secondary cognitive dissonance

Art Linkletter gained a large audience with a segment on his afternoon television show, "House Party," called "Kids Say the Darndest Things." Would-be consolers say the damnedest things—words that have a long *shelf life*.

You might ask, "How do people suggest to you that it is time you *move on* or *get over* N___'s death?"

Yes, some in the grief patrol use trumpets and trombones to communicate their message, but the same intent can be communicated with oboes and bassoons. Follow up with, "How do you handle those comments?" or "How do you wish you could respond to such comments?"

Post-suicide grievers need to be encouraged to be bold in responding to a "Move on!" directive, "May I tell you how what you just said sounds to me?"

Know solid readable books on grief

There are lots of books on grief but few that specifically focus on suicide. Early in grief, grievers need what I call *griever-friendly* reading. For that reason, I have written several books with two-page chapters. I am stunned when authors write long chapters and when publishers use small font and pack too many words on a page. The words blur.

If your budget permits, give copies of books grievers have told you they found helpful. Book recommendations are wonderful, but many grievers do not follow-through. If you place the book in their hands or even point to a particular passage, the griever is more likely to read it—and to *keep* reading.

You may qualify a grief book, "Now, some grievers have told me that this has been a helpful resource. You, however, *might not* find it helpful. So please be sure to let me know your opinion!"

You may protest, *I don't have time to read all the books on grief.* Then enlist grievers to read for you and make recommendations.

Be aware that some grief books, particularly written by fundamentalist Christians, are heavy on theological focus or rely on the outdated "stages of grief." Some have a *hidden* agenda. I cannot name all the books with some variation of this format:

"My spouse suicided."
"Jesus/God helped me *get over it* or *move on.*"
"I am over my grief and back to normal."
"I turned my grief over to God," which signals, *so should you!*

Some books with a distinctly Christian view of grief are widely recommended. However, what about landmines within the book? Other books suggest *reincarnation light.*

When invited to speak to groups of grievers, remember diversity

I was invited to speak at a December remembrance service for suicide survivors. In my preparation, I reminded myself, *how will this point be heard by individuals who are present or heard by those who do not come from a Christian tradition or who are atheists?*

During the cookies-and-punch time after the program, a woman approached me, "Thank you for your sensitivity that not everyone here is Christian. In past years, some speakers have . . . "

This particular grieving mother was Jewish and found my words comforting.

Engage in long-haul pastoral presence

Many clergy are good for short-haul pastoral care in the immediacy following the death. Are you prepared and committed to doing on-going involvement with grievers as they attempt to assimilate the loss into their narrative? *Reverend, I have been thinking about something you said.* I want to believe that the funeral/memorial service is for seed-planting, not harvesting!

For example, following the suicide of a high school student, the family may appear to be coping. They may dodge questions by saying pointedly, *we are doing fine. Thank you for asking. It was hard at the beginning. We are doing better.* However, prom night or graduation may evoke a fresh crisis when grievers are confronted by a brutal reality, *my son/daughter is not here to participate in this rite of passage*—or in the fall, when friends/neighbor's children head off to college. Be available for event-generated counseling following weddings, retirements, fiftieth anniversaries, birth of first grandchild.

Be alert to the iceberg syndrome

Be alert to the iceberg floating in the sea of grief. Thanatologist and author Ben Wolfe uses a wonderful analogy of grief as an iceberg. Our vision is drawn to the part of the iceberg *above* the waterline. We may conclude or even compliment, *you are doing so well.* Wolfe, after working with hundreds of grievers, notes that only ten percent of an iceberg is above the water; ninety percent is below. I often inform grievers, *it is* not *the ten percent above the water line that threatens the ship.*

In working with a family, listen in. and you may hear a tip-off about issues within the individual or the family that are in the shadowy waters below the surface—issues that are complicating the integration of the suicide.

I have on occasion shown a picture of an iceberg as a prop to transmit this analogy. Weeks later, some grievers have said, *I've been thinking about that picture of the iceberg you showed me . . .*

Be alert to shattering post-suicide discoveries

Some families I have worked with have been stunned—if not ambushed—by post-suicide discoveries. Some mates, spouses, partners, parents, family members *pretend* not to know certain things, or they dowse their suspicions. You will, at some point, have *the other* in the deceased's life show up at a visitation or funeral. Others feel humiliated for being *the last one to know*.

Upon arriving in Warm Springs, Georgia in April, 1945, just hours after the death of her husband, President Franklin D. Roosevelt, Eleanor asked a simple question that would complicate her grief, "Who was here *when* Franklin died?"

She was informed that his two cousins, his valet, the Secretary of the Treasury, Secret Service agents, and his physician had been present, but for some reason, Eleanor asked, "Anyone else?"

Franklin's cousin, Laura Delano, responded, "She was here."

"*She. She who?*" Eleanor asked.

"Lucy was here,"—Lucy Mercer Rutherfurd, who Franklin had promised Eleanor in 1918 to give up after their affair became known.

"That is not possible," Eleanor protested. "Franklin promised he would never see her again."

"Well, he *may* have promised you that, but she had been here for three days."

Eleanor stood and walked into the small bedroom where the corpse lay and shut the door. She remained in the room for five minutes. I wish I knew what she said. She sat up all night on the funeral train staring out the window at the large crowds that lined the eight hundred miles of railroad track back to Washington. She had to act as if she were a poor grieving widow when, in reality, she was angry! Franklin had betrayed her again! Soon, she learned Lucy had been with Franklin on several occasions in her absence in the White House. Moreover, she learned that her daughter Anna had managed the necessary arrangements for the visits. But this was 1945! Who could Eleanor speak to—certainly not the minister who conducted the funeral.[2]

A question for pastors

I have borrowed from my colleague-friend, Dr. Frank Freed, a clinician in California, a question that you might use.

2. Goodwin, *No Ordinary time*, 611–612

Freed asked clients, "*What* are you pretending not to know about?"

Some initially seemed puzzled by his question; he repeats the question with a different emphasis, "What are *you* pretending not to know about this suicide?"

The question, for some, has led to a breakthrough moment in pastoral care.

Offer makom hanekhama

Offer a safe place of comfort to grievers. So many suicide grievers function like castles surrounded by a moat, only they have drawn up the bridge. There is no way into the castle or out of the castle. The only thing I promise grievers in my groups at Saint Luke's Hospital is that I will do my best to provide *makom hanekhama* (a place of comfort) or a safe place for them to grieve. This has been particularly beneficial to LGBT grievers and for individuals who have issues they would feel uncomfortable sharing with a pastor, priest, or rabbi.

Following a suicide, a griever may need a safe place to sort through ideas, notions, perceptions, false beliefs. *I thought we had a great marriage, so why would he end his life? Or I promised "in sickness and in health." Did he think I would desert him after his cancer diagnosis?*

It may not be in the first pastoral visit or second pastoral visit, but at some point, a griever may conclude that you are *safe*, and they can unload psychological and/or spiritual wounds that have complicated their grief.

Know examples of individuals that have died by suicide

That also means knowing how their families have incorporated the loss. NFL football coach and television football commentator Tony Dungy's son Tony, 18, suicided three days before Christmas, 2005. The owners of the Indianapolis Colts, bound for the post-season, told Dungy to take as much time as he needed. He did do not have to come back to coach during the post-season. Ten days later, Colts fans and others via television coverage noticed Coach Dungy on the sidelines calling plays.

Wow, no few football fans said, *he's back!* For some, the implication was that, if Tony Dungy can *move on*—or, more likely, appear to have moved on—after his young son's suicide, so should you! Within six weeks, Dungy spoke at a pre-Super Bowl breakfast for Athletes in Action about the lessons he had learned, i.e., in six weeks! Later, Dungy expanded his thoughts in a biography—a distinctly evangelical Christian biography:

> He was a Christian and is today in heaven. He was struggling with the things of the world and took his own life. People ask how I could come back to work so soon. I'm not totally recovered, I don't know if I ever will be, it's still ever-painful," he said, wiping back a tear. "But some good things have come out of it."

> To the hushed audience, Dungy raised this question, "Why does God allow pain in our life?" Dungy answered, "Because we're loved by God and the pain allows us to head back to our Father."[3]

That worked for Tony Dungy. I would have been more appreciative if he had waited to speak publicly and had given time for his grief to *set up*. His memoir, *Quiet Strength,* became a bestseller. One father who was given the book—after his son's death—was livid! *He hasn't begun to deal with the grief.*

Encourage memoir

Years ago, memoirs were written by well-known individuals, politicians, celebrities, or sport figures. In recent years, the field has blossomed and in some circles is now called, "life-writing." A biography or autobiography covers a whole life or a life *lived so far.* The memoir is narrower: It focuses on a particular segment of time.

I have developed a process I call "en-training" to help grievers write memoir.[4] Imagine a freight train. The engine of the train is the suicide death. I ask grievers to add three page, double spaced "boxcars" to that engine. Some suicide survivors want to write a book. That is noble, but actually writing it is a challenge. But if the goal can be divided into three-page memoir *slices*, writing a book becomes more possible. Indeed, the effort may never be published, but the writing process—that string of box-cars—adds clarity to the grieving process. What the griever has written and shared with friends or family may offer a *bridge* into understanding one's grief or facilitating conversations.

I ask grievers to start with simple non-threatening themes for a memoir slice:

---

3. Stricklin, *The Baptist Press,* February 3, 2016
4. Smith, *Techniques of grief therapy,* 237–239

What was N___'s favorite flavor of ice cream?

What was N___'s idea of a great midnight snack?

What was something N___ said that drove you nuts?

What did N___'s laugh sound like?

What adjectives would describe N___?

What was one philosophy of life which N___ held most important?

These initial jump starter memoir slices often convince the griever, *I can do this.* Sometimes, I ask grievers to revisit a segment of writing to see how they would now answer the question.

Some grievers have been surprised that they wrote something funny or that produced a tear when reading it. Some report that writing on one of these *safe* questions had resulted in another question popping in their mind, *I hadn't thought of this in years.*

Encourage poetry writing

Through the Western canon of literature, there is a large body of "death/ grief" poetry—some syrupy, some irritating, some inane, like "Don't Stand at My Grave and Weep." Really? For 18 years at St. Luke's—and with individual grievers—I have urged them to write poems. To encourage that process, I give them the first line, *grief came knocking at my door one day.* I ask the griever to write four lines but insist that it does *not* have to rhyme! I suggest before picking up the pen or pencil, turn that phrase over and over in their minds (like clothes tumbling in a dryer), *grief came knocking at my door one day, grief came knocking at my door one day,* then write whatever comes to mind.

I ask, "Would you be willing to read your poem to me?"

Offering hospitality to *that* poem—or to that poetic effort—is critical. Sometimes I ask, "Would you read that again?"

Sometimes, the poem—of whatever quality—has become a diving board into a meaningful conversation on the death or their grief. Urge grievers to share the poem with someone because it may jumpstart that individual's thinking and feeling, grieving and remembering. Another grief root line I offer is, *I keep hoping that one of these days.*

At times, given the prominence of poetry by Helen S. Rice, I ask if they know Mrs. Rice's occupation. Of course, I get *poet.* I explain that she was a professional lamp shade designer and marketing specialist but began writing down her thoughts after the suicide death of her husband. By putting her words down on paper, Helen Stiner Rice has offered comfort to millions of individuals.[5]

Know skilled clinicians in your community

Not every mental health professional or chaplain, rabbi or minister is *good* with grief. Some are not good listeners or not good at offering hospitality to rambling grief narratives—they prefer to cut to the chase. Some have their own death anxiety or unaddressed grief issues. Ask around as to who has the best reputation for being a compassionate human being who listens to suicide mourners.

Secondly, what is the counselor's fee structure? Grief counseling may be a *luxury* given new financial circumstances that grievers find themselves in. I often explain that grief counseling is an investment, not an expenditure.

You might want to talk to a clinician or counselor over coffee and invite them to give you an overview of their understanding of grief or how they work with grievers, particularly suicide survivors.

If they offer you the five stages of grief, this is not the counselor for you to recommend! If the counselor thinks grief is something to be *gotten over* rather than *gotten into*, this is not a candidate for referral.

Remember the red letter days on the griever's personal calendars

Individuals are good at sending initial condolence cards during the first days or week or month following a suicide. They may, however, be frustrated in trying to find the *right* card given the circumstances of the death (the greeting card companies have overlooked this niche of the grief market.) Lesser are the grievers who receive cards at thirty days, sixty days, but particularly on the anniversary of the suicide. To be honest, I often use cards that are blank on the inside. Recently, I realized the anniversary of a friend's talented young son's suicide was approaching. I found a card with a picture of hands holding a tiny baby. On the inside of the card, I wrote, "Once you have held them, you *always* hold them." I struggled because the

5. Pollitt and Wiltse, *Helen Stiner Rice*

father of the deceased is a brilliant hospital chaplain who had worked with many grievers over his career. What if he found my card a little hokey?

I received an email. Thank you for the card. Your words were exactly "right on"—you *cannot* let them go. Then he wrote: "With the busy schedule you have, it meant a lot that you would think of us at this time."

Pay attention to that year of firsts: *first* birthday, *first* anniversary, *first* graduation, *first* prom night, etc. But also, remember seconds and thirds. Often, I have sent a simple card with these words, "Thinking of you *today*, knowing that today is a red letter day on the calendar of your heart." I have been surprised by mothers who have told me, *you remembered!* I have been saddened by others who said, *you are the only one of his friends who remembered*. Yes, you are busy, and it is easy to forget, so have your secretary or someone in the congregation be assigned to remind you of this important aspect of ministry.

Show up. Keep showing up.

Ninety-one point two (91.2) percent of pastoral care for grievers is about presence and availability. Post-suicide pastoral care is not rocket-science but compassionate presence.

Post-suicide pastoral care is *not* about knowing what to say; truth be told, sometimes there is nothing to say.

Post-suicide pastoral care is about listening—and listening some more—and listening to some things a second and third time. It is possible on the twentieth telling, a piece of the puzzle slips into place, and you share an *ah-ha* moment with a griever.

Anticipate an "intersection" moment

Edwin Shneidman, PhD, was the founder of Suicidology as an academic discipline and did much during his long career to empower professionals to destigmatize suicide. In a funeral/memorial service following a suicide or during a pastoral care opportunity, I like to tell a story about Dr. Shneidman being asked to share a few words at a gathering of mental health professionals. The host of the event had been clear, *brief* remarks. Shneidman was called to the podium and looked out at the large audience. He thanked the host for the invitation to "share a few words."

Taking a breath, the psychologist announced, "I have discovered two questions, which if asked, would lower the suicide rate in this country. Thank you very much for your attention."

Shneidman turned to walk back to his seat. The audience would not have it!

"What are the questions?" individuals began to shout. "Tell us the two questions!"

The chair broke into a sweat.

Dr. Shneidman chose to enjoy the moment by protesting, "No. I could not possibly take any more time away from our main speaker. You came to hear the speaker, *not* me."

The audience demanded that Shneidman clarify his remarks. Finally, he stepped back to the podium.

"The two questions that would lower the suicide rate in this country are," he paused, "One, *where do you hurt* and two, *how can I help you?*"

The major speaker faced an audience pondering Shneidman's questions, not his presentation.[6]

Clergy can borrow Shneidman's questions (and the story). Keep the two questions cued up for an encounter with suicide grievers.

"There are two questions I would like to ask you. Think a moment before answering."

"*Where* do you hurt?"

"*How* can I help you?"

No, the deceased cannot be brought *back to life*, but one can utilize the mumbling, *I wish I had* or *if only I had* to reach out to others facing a similar constellation of psychological stress. Clergy can urge—admonish—grievers to offer hospitality to the psychological pain that is reality for so many in our world—a pain, Shneidman believes, convinces the sufferer there is only one way to end the pain, suicide.

Edwin Shneidman's research convinced him that most individuals do not want to die. They do, however, want the pain to end and cannot think of any other way to end that pain.

I suggest a third question for clergy to answer, "How willing am I to be inconvenienced by the individual's answers to questions one and two?"

I would expect that question to irritate some readers, "Does he have any idea how overworked I am? I already have a to-do list a mile long. I am running behind as soon as I get out of bed in the morning."

---

6. Shneidman, *Suicide & Life-Threatening Behavior*, 8

Jesus stunned his disciples by asking a question after they grumbled about finding him talking to a woman.

He asked, "Do you see *this* woman?"[7] Young clergy feel pressured to appear busy, always look busy.

Jesus did not ask, "Do you see *these* women?"

One pastor I know—who is not into grief care—was recently asked in a congregational meeting, "What exactly do you do all day?"

I wondered the same question. To his credit, he delivers an excellent sermon on many Sunday mornings.

Balancing impossible demands, particularly in a one-clergy community of faith, is maddening. Still, the question remains, *do you see* this *griever?*

I suggest three broader questions:

"What can *this* griever teach me about life after suicide?"

"What can *this* griever teach me about offering helpful pastoral presence and care following a suicide?"

"What can this griever teach me about who I really am and what should be important in my life?"

Borrowing a Prayer

I appreciate the prayer of Sister Joan Chittister, "God, where are you in *this?*"[8] I loan that easy-to-memorize prayer to suicide grievers. Because you are clergy—particularly if you are considered *safe* clergy—the question may be directed to you, *where was/where is God in this?* And, in all probability, your response will be quoted.

Borrow sacred text

Given the religious diversity in American culture, I often borrow from other traditions. The old adage applied to weddings, *something old, something new; something borrowed, something blue*, applies to rituals following suicide. I recommend the following prayer to individuals or to include in the service, sometimes to be read responsively or printed in the funeral program. I call this prayer, "The Griever's Petition for Reconciliation."

7. Luke 7:44, NIV
8. Chittister, Lecture

All that we ought to have thought
and have not thought,
All that we ought to have said,
and have not said,
All that we ought to have done,
and have not done;
All that we ought not to have thought,
and yet have thought.
All that we ought not to have spoken,
and yet have spoken.
All that we ought not to have done,
and yet have done;
For thoughts, words and works,
pray we, O God, for forgiveness.

– "The Naming of Names," St. Luke's Hospital, Kansas City, Missouri

Sometimes, after I have read the text aloud, I ask, "What is left out of this prayer?" I may nudge by repeating a couple of phrases, "What I said that I should not have said . . . what I did that I should not have done."

Then I share a snippet of the prayer's history. These words were framed by the Zoroastrians in Persia 2,700 years ago. For twenty-seven centuries, individuals have found meaning in reciting or reflecting on these words. Perhaps you can too.

Encourage organ donation

After a suicide death, some individuals cling to a cliché as if it were a life vest, *something good will come out of this*. In some cases, a family—when death is not immediate—give permission for organ donation. The Dungys, for example, delayed a postmortem to facilitate organ donation. So, out of a horrible godawful moment, someone got the gift of life through a heart, a lung, a cornea, skin, tissue, or a liver.

I tell individuals: "You have a choice about the last line on N___'s life resume. It can be *died by suicide*, but you have the right to alter or ameliorate the last line of that resume with *organ donor*. How do you wish to remember the end of your loved one's life?"

I have wondered the impact on my family narrative if my father could have received a kidney transplant.

Be a gap-stander

The Hebrew scripture contains a story about God looking "for someone among them who would . . . stand before me in the gap."[9]

In early days of pastoral service, you can expect to hear—probably more than once—and sometimes dowsed in anger, "*You* don't understand."

Someone may demand, "So, have *you* ever had a family member die by suicide?"

Sadly, I answer, "Yes. Too many."

But, if that is not your experience, you might answer, "You are right. I do not understand. *But* I will never understand if you do not talk to me and stretch my understanding."

The irony, you may be most effectively tutored by a griever following a suicide.

Clergy have an opportunity, particularly following a death by suicide, to stand in the gap and offer hope. Clergy can encourage others to invite some serious reflection. In a sense, clergy have an opportunity to give the individual back to family, friends, neighbors. Pastoral care should be viewed as an opportunity to plant *seeds* that may take years to bloom in some lives.

Often, following a death by suicide, people of faith struggle with praying.

"Why pray?" one father snarled. "Why didn't God protect him from himself?"

Some are hesitant to share with a spiritual leader their questions about the effectiveness of prayer. Sometimes, I ask grievers if they might be open to *borrowing* a prayer—an easy-to-remember prayer.

Rabbi David Wolpe of Los Angeles is a hero of mine. I give them a thumbnail of Rabbi Wolpe's battle with leukemia, then I quote his prayer, "God, stay close."[10] Sometimes, I encourage the griever to punctuate the prayer with an exclamation or two!

9. Ezekiel 22:30 NIV
10. Grossman, *USA Today*

Preparation for pastoral care

In preparing for an opportunity to offer pastoral presence and pastoral care following a death by suicide, clergy would wisely invest in moments praying or reflecting on the prayer of Francis of Assisi:

> Lord, make us instruments of your peace.
> Where there is hatred, let us sow love;
> Where there is injury, pardon;
> Where there is discord, union;
> Where there is doubt, faith;
> Where there is despair, hope;
> Where there is darkness, light;
> Where there is sadness, joy;
> O Divine Master, Grant that we may not so much seek
> To be consoled as to console,
> To be understood as to understand,
> To be loved as to love.
> For it is in giving that we receive;
> It is in pardoning that we are pardoned;
> And it is in dying that we are born to eternal life.
> Amen.

Conclusion

William Gladstone, British prime minister, observed, "Show me the manner in which a nation cares for its dead, and I will measure with mathematical exactness the tender mercies of its people, their respect for the laws of the land and their loyalty to high ideals."[11]

I would ask you to ponder this paraphrase, "Show me the manner in which *a community of faith* cares for its grieving *following a suicide*, and I will measure with mathematical exactness the tender mercies of its people and its leadership."

Often the best *help* is simply showing up—and showing up some more.

---

11. Gladstone, *The American Cemetery* 13

Bibliography

Chittister, Joan. Lecture. Country Club Christian Church. Kansas City, Missouri, November 9, 2009.

Gladstone, William E. "Successful cemetery advertising." *The American Cemetery*, March, 1938, p. 13.

Goodwin, Doris Kearns. *No ordinary time: Franklin & Eleanor Roosevelt: The home front in World War II*. New York: Simon & Schuster, 1994.

Grossman, Cathy Lynn. "Rabbi Wolpe's "faith" takes on atheists and fanatics alike." *USA Today*, September 22, 2008. Electronic version.

Holy Bible: New International Version. London: Hodder & Stoughton, 1979.

Pollitt, Ronald, and Virginia Wiltse. *Helen Steiner Rice: Ambassador of sunshine*. Grand Rapids, MI: F.H. Revell, 1994.

Shneidman, Edwin S. "Suicidology and the university: A founder's reflections at 80." *Suicide and Life-Threatening Behavior* 31, no. 1 (2001): 1–8.

Smith, Harold Ivan. "En training." In *Techniques of grief therapy: Creative practices for counseling the bereaved*, Robert A. Neimeyer, ed. New York: Routledge, 2012, 237–239.

Stricklin, Art. "Tony Dungy Voices the Pain & Lessons from His Son's Suicide." *Baptist Press*. February 3, 2006. Accessed August 03, 2016. http://www.bpnews.net/22595/tony-dungy-voices-the-pain-and-lessons-from-his-sons-suicide.

For additional reading

Smith, Harold Ivan. *A long-shadowed grief: Suicide and its aftermath*. Cambridge, MA: Cowley Press, 2006.

———. *A Decembered Grief: Gift edition*. Kansas City, MO: Beacon Hill Press, 2011.

———. *When a child you know is grieving*. (Rev. ed.). Kansas City, MO: Beacon Hill Press, 2012.

———. *When you don't know what to say*. (Rev. ed.).Kansas City, MO: Beacon Hill Press, 2012.

Some Suggested Resources

Anderson, Linda. *First Tears Over the Loss of your Child.* Chicago, IL: ACTA Publications, 2009.

Chance, Sue. *Stronger than Death: When Suicide Touches Your Life.* New York, NY: W. W. Norton & Company, 1997.

Chatman, Delle and William Kenneally. *The Death of a Parent: Reflections for Adults Mourning the Loss of a Father or Mother.* Chicago, IL: ACTA Publications, 2003.

Fine, Carla. *No Time to Say Goodbye: Surviving the Suicide of a Loved One.* New York: Broadway Books, 2011.

Fitzgerald, William John. *Words of Comfort: What to Say at Times of Sadness or Loss.* Phoenix, AZ: Tau Publishing, 1999.

Grollman, Earl. *Living When a Loved One Has Died* (rev. ed.). London: Souvenir Press, 2014.

Grollman, Earl. *Living When a Young Friend Commits Suicide (Or Even Starts Talking about It).* Boston, MA: Beacon Press, 1999.

Hoy, William G. and J. William Worden. *Do Funerals Matter? The Purpose and Practices of Death Rituals in Global Perspective.* New York: Routledge, 2013.

Jaworski, Katrina. *The Gender of Suicide: Knowledge Production, Theory and Suicidology.* Burlington, VT: Ashgate, 2014.

Joiner, Thomas. *Why People Die by Suicide.* Boston, MA: Harvard University Press, 2005.

Mason, Karen. *Preventing Suicide: A Handbook for Pastors, Chaplains, and Pastoral Counselors.* Downers Grove, IL: IVP Books, an imprint of InterVarsity, 2014.

Rubel, Barbara. *But I Didn't Say Goodbye: Helping Children and Families After a Suicide.* Kendall Park, NJ: Griefwork Center, 1999.

Spexarth, Kristen. *Passing Reflections, Vol. III, Revised and Expanded: Surviving Suicide Loss through Mindfulness.* San Francisco, CA: Big Think Media, 2016.

Stillwell, Elaine. *The Death of a Child: Reflections for Grieving Parents.* Chicago, IL: ACTA Publications, 2004. (Advice to Grieving Parents)